Shadows in the Bricks

The old shops of South Bank in York

CLEMENTS HALL LOCAL HISTORY GROUP

2019

Published in 2019 by

Clements Hall Local History Group
Clements Hall, Nunthorpe Road, York YO23 1BW

www.clementshallhistorygroup.org.uk

Other publications from the Group:

Bishy Road: a York shopping street in time

Clements Hall Local History Group was founded in 2013. Members of the Group have wide-ranging interests in the local history of their neighbourhood – the Clementhorpe, Scarcroft and South Bank areas of York, to the south of the city walls and west of the River Ouse.

ISBN 978-1-9996655-1-7

Typesetting by Lesley Collett

Printed by B & B Press, Rotherham

Contents

Sources and acknowledgements

Our researches into the history of the old shops of South Bank began almost as soon as we launched our Group in 2013. Carol Warren carried out some very useful work, interviewing local residents, and we started to collect data. Since then we have drawn upon the memories and records of a number of local people, an invaluable foundation for this book, in particular the late Derrick Gray, Kevin Horner and David Meek. We are most grateful for the willingness of local residents to share their information and memories, which we displayed at our exhibition at The Winning Post in 2016.

Further research has drawn upon many archival sources: census records, trade directories, maps, contemporary newspaper accounts, council records and advertisements in church magazines. Sadly the current inaccessibility of original City Engineers plans in the City Archives has once again prevented us from a thorough investigation of land ownership and building plans in the area.

In addition to my own research, interviews and directory research have been carried out by other History Group members, in particular Anne Houson, Anne Bush, Sue Popel and Pauline Alden. Dick Hunter and Meredith Andrea provided supportive comments and Rob Stay has shared his researches into 'Count' de Burgh. More recently Keith Watson has kindly shared his extensive records and images of South Bank and helped with investigations.

Other contributors have included Mike Pollard and his father John, Peter Stanhope, Clare Bryant, Marion Goodrick, Joan Jackman, Jean Potts, the late Hugh Murray, Christine Studstrop, Karen Thompson, Dennis Job, Emma Davis, Carole Smith, Barbara Weatherley, Vikki O'Brien, Nigel Scurr, Ken and Linda Haywood, Peter Stanhope, Andrew Franks, Charles and Gill Symington, Alison Sinclair, Geoff Shearsmith, Brian Hughes, Simon Batchelor, Hazel Morrill, Christine Gajewicz and her mother Gillian Shuttleworth, Haresh Patel, Geoff Turner, Catrina Appleby, Colette Cross, Diane Lewis, Gill Chambers, Malcolm and Fiona Tolladay, and Fred Thomas. My apologies to anyone I have left out.

Giles Cookson from The Card Index has been very obliging, and John Shaw, Sandra Garside-Neville and Ian Drake from YAYAS have contributed much help and advice. We are also grateful to the City Archives at York Explore (especially Julie-Anne Vickers) and the Borthwick Archive, for their invaluable resources.

The funding awarded for our previous book, from Bishopthorpe Road Traders Association, Micklegate Ward Fund, The Noel Goddard Terry Charitable Trust and the Yorkshire Architectural and York Archaeological Society (YAYAS), has enabled us to use the income from sales of that book to publish our current research, and so we are most grateful to them once again.

This account is as accurate as possible but we apologise for any errors, which we hope to correct on our website at www.clementshallhistorygroup.org.uk.

Susan Major
Clements Hall Local History Group

NUNTHORPE HALL

View of Nunthorpe Hall from the conservatory side, overlooking the Knavesmire. (Geoff Shearsmith)

The grocer's shop on the corner of Butcher Terrace and Bishopthorpe Rd around 1913. (Hugh Murray)

Introduction

Ever wondered about features of our South Bank neighbourhood, such as why there are so many bricked up shops, why some groups of houses are different to their neighbours, and why certain street corners have a different shape? Have you noticed that many of the streets have historical names? Did you know that some well-known music acts played their early gigs here, and the tradition continues? And who was Count de Burgh? These are traces of our history, leaving an indelible mark on South Bank.

It's a popular area of York, attractive to young families because of its location, its schools and green spaces. South Bank is a densely packed area of housing bordering the Bishopthorpe Rd as it travels southwards. To the north is Southlands Rd, set on a ridge, to the east is the river Ouse, to the south are Bustardthorpe allotments and open countryside, while York Racecourse is to the west.

Most housing here dates from the late 19th century/early 20th century, with long straight streets of small houses opening directly onto pavements, although some have small forecourts. These were built by developers 100 years ago, to make money out of land. They housed artisans and other workers who needed housing near to the new factories. The exception is the Nunthorpe estate of red-brick semi-detached houses, built in the 1930s on a plot of land in the middle of the area, and sadly suffering devastating damage during World War II.

These streets are now lined with cars. While built for the working classes, housing here has become more expensive as a result of York's housing economy, restricted by the rise of housing as an investment rather than a basic need. Long-standing resident families, knitted together as a community by local churches, pubs, schools, working men's and sports clubs, are now replaced often by shorter-term tenants. But the area still has a very friendly community feel, as people inevitably meet on the streets.

Over the last 100 years South Bank has been a surprising hot spot for all kinds of shops, over a hundred, at a time when people shopped locally rather than in the city centre, either walking or cycling to their local traders. These were part of the local community and well-known and remembered. People have fond memories of a barber who used to sit on his front doorstep serenading on his banjo, of street parties and Coronation celebrations. The area is still interlaced with back alleyways, featuring traditional and distinctive stone paviours, and people talk about the local sloping alleyways, some known as 'the sleepers'. They remember milk delivered in jugs on doorsteps, grocers using a horse and cart for deliveries and children taking ages to choose penny sweets at the sweet shop.

But very few shops remain, driven out by competition from supermarkets and the availability of personal motor transport. As you walk along these streets however you can spot the traces of shops, often houses with oblique bricked-up corners and the bricked-up remains of flat display windows, leaving just shadows in the bricks.

Moments in history

A map of York from 1852, surveyed by Captain Tucker, shows empty fields below the old 1820s terraces around the city walls to the south of the city. On the west bank of the River Ouse there is very little below Clementhorpe, just the remains of St Clement's Church and Nunnery, and a few industrial buildings such as Clementhorpe Dye Works, taking advantage of the river.

The church and surrounding lands had been part of St. Clement's Nunnery, founded in 1130 and the first nunnery to be established in the North of England after the Norman Conquest. But it was suppressed in 1536, and the church later merged with the parish of St. Mary Bishophill Senior in 1585. In the late 19th century, the last Rector of the united parishes, the Revd. George Marsham Argles (later Canon of York) pushed for a separate church to serve the parish, which was growing faster than any other in York, and the foundation stone of St. Clement's Church was laid in 1871.

The area south of what is now Southlands Rd, an area we now call South Bank, was formerly known as Nun Ings and Nunthorpe. The 1852 map shows only the Nun Windmill (sited on a high ridge where Southlands Church is now) and Campleshon Pond, which was near a narrow lane – Campleshon Lane. The pond was a flooded early gravel pit in the area now at the lower end of Trafalgar Street. There were surprisingly a couple of newly built semi-detached early Victorian villas with ornate gardens, labelled 'Nunthorpe', on the east side of Bishopthorpe Rd, to the south of what is now Beresford Terrace, and backing onto the river. Nun Ings is still largely intact today.

The Nun Windmill was on a mound, one of several around the city, which served to house batteries during the Parliamentary Siege on York in 1644. The site has another surprising claim to fame, as it was said to be where Archbishop Richard Scrope was beheaded, after playing a leading role in the northern uprising against Henry IV in 1405. Skaife's map of 1864 shows this to be the site of Richard Scrope's Chapel, although his tomb and the Scrope Chapel are now at York Minster.

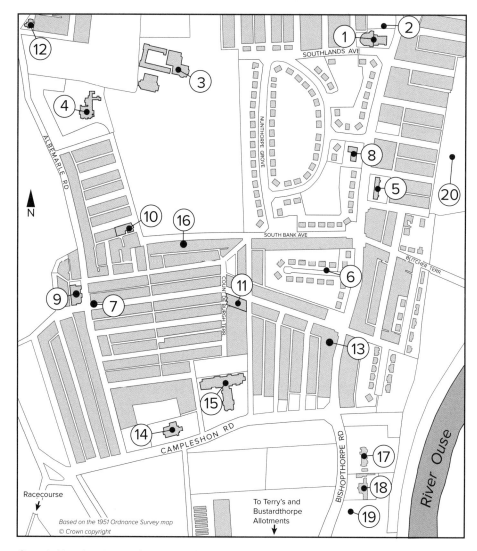

South Bank: sites of principal buildings

1. Southlands Methodist Church
2. Site of Windmill and Scrope chapel
3. Nunthorpe Court (now part of Millthorpe School)
4. Site of Nunthorpe Hall
5. Cameron Walker Homes
6. St Clement's Rectory site
7. Old tram terminus
8. 'The Winning Post' pub
9. 'The Knavesmire' pub
10. South Bank Social Club
11. St Clement's WMC
12. Kentmere House
13. South Bank Medical Centre
14. St Chad's
15. Knavesmire Primary School
16. Old South Bank Mission Chapel (now private house)
17. Site of Old Nunthorpe
18. Site of Riverside Lodge
19. Site of Ashcroft
20. Rowntree Park

The mill was one of two medieval windmills in 1524 belonging to Isabella Ward, Prioress of St Clement's Nunnery, and built during the Nunnery's existence. It appears on Archer's map of York in 1680, and on Lund's map in 1772. (Another mill at Holgate had been built in 1770). David Hicks Wilstrop arrived as miller from Rufforth Mill in 1830 and then moved on to Castle Mills in 1843, to be replaced by his brother Thomas, who sadly later died of cholera in 1854. Ironically the following year a doctor born in York, Dr Snow, published his findings on how cholera was transmitted, using the experience of the Broad Street water pump in London.

The last miller was George Plummer, and the mill was eventually demolished in 1880, to make way for a new Methodist chapel and houses. During demolition work Civil War cannonballs and lead musket bullets were found nearby. In 1981 a deep sewer excavation in Bishopthorpe Rd noted a compact layer of Roman road cobbles, some two metres below the modern road level.

Railways and chocolate

It was railways and chocolate that encouraged the development of housing in South Bank towards the end of the 19th century. The coming of the railway to York in 1839 generated a need for worker housing. This was not only for the large number of new railway workers, there were now many more opportunities for goods and people to travel between York and other parts of the country, expanding employment opportunities. The North Eastern Railway carriage and wagon works opened at Holgate in 1867. Confectionery manufacturer Joseph Terry and Sons had moved to new steam-powered premises in Clementhorpe in 1864, giving the factory access to the Humber estuary and the North Sea. The York Confectionery Co., founded in Fossgate in 1867, moved to Fenwick St, off Bishopthorpe Rd, specialising in candied peel and mint rock supplied to many seaside resorts.

With the opening of the Skeldergate Bridge over the Ouse in 1881, South Bank was a prime candidate for space to meet the large demand for housing. Before then those wanting to cross the River Ouse from the centre of York towards Bishopthorpe had to use the ferry at Skeldergate Postern. It had been a busy service, with over 800 people reported to be using the boat each day around this time. The area south of the river was already a rapidly growing community and the bridge supported much new housing in the last twenty years of the 19th century.

The first part of South Bank to be built on was to the north west with four small terraced streets built around 1881: Adelaide St, Argyle St, Windsor St and the south side of Philadelphia Terrace. A little later Albemarle Terrace was built, the northern end of what was to become a key trading street, Albemarle Rd.

A few men played a key role in the shaping of the South Bank we know today. 'Count' de Burgh was a major developer, owning large areas of land which he sold for housing, another was John Thomas Wood. Press reports at the turn of the 20th century refer to three estates: Bishopthorpe Rd, with 210 houses, and a further 300 being erected or planned, the Nunthorpe estate by the river, with 38 houses built and 22 in progress, and the South Bank estate, with 150 houses built. By 1903 there were 628 occupied houses in the three estates, with 712 by 1904 and 785 by 1905.

A local brewery company, John J Hunt Ltd, made several attempts to open public houses in this developing area, despite strong religious opposition from Canon Argles, who prevented the building of public houses for many years in this area, because of his strong temperance views. In 1900 there was an unsuccessful application from the brewery for a full licence for premises at the west end of South Bank Ave. As well as religious opponents there were complaints from a local off-licence shopkeeper, Mr Jackson, in Adelaide St, worried about competition. But local people suggested that otherwise there was only the Club and the Knavesmire Grandstand, and that 'women should not have to go across a common in the winter months to get brandy or anything else from the Grandstand'. It was unsuccessful. Argles had strong views, he also refused to allow his parish to be divided into two churches while he was alive, despite the growing population of South Bank, relying on mission halls instead.

Bishopthorpe Rd looking south from Richardson St, 1911.

The slightly grander streets on the eastern side of Bishopthorpe Rd were mainly completed by the early 1900s, for example Bewlay St (1879), Richardson St (1881), Beresford Terrace and Terry St (1900), Butcher Terrace and Finsbury St (1900), Norfolk St (1912), St Clement's Grove (1912), Aldreth Grove (1912), Cameron Grove (1912), Finsbury Ave (1936). Work was carried out at various times to widen Bishopthorpe Rd in 1905 and the 1920s. In 1925 there was a plan to build a continuation of Campleshon Rd to Heslington via a river bridge, as part of a proposed new inner ring road, but this failed due to a lack of government funding.

Southlands Rd was set on a high ridge of land, facing south, between Russell St and Nunmill St, on what used to be the drive up to Nunthorpe Court. It had two blocks of large three storey houses, built in 1893. In modern times a few of these houses have been converted into guest houses because of their size, and there has been some infill, with more recent housing towards the west end of the road, when in 1937 the eastern gateway to Nunthorpe Court was closed and land made available for housing.

Queen Victoria St around 1900, with the grocer on the corner. (YAYAS)

By 1907 the terraced streets were gradually being built up in the southern part of the area. These celebrated the Victorian era with their names, following the Queen's Diamond Jubilee ten years previously in 1897. Brunswick St and Queen Victoria St were almost fully built up, but Balmoral Terrace was only partly developed. Much of Knavesmire Crescent now contained houses, and the east side of Curzon Terrace. Much of the west side of Albemarle Rd was built up, but there were still allotment gardens on the east side. South Bank Ave was originally the entrance driveway to a big house, Nunthorpe Hall, to the north of Philadelphia Terrace. It now featured houses along most of its southern side, these were semi-detached houses, with pointed, half-timber gables, and a row of terraced houses. Other streets with a limited number of houses were Kensington St, Montague St, Trafalgar St, Count de Burgh Terrace and Sutherland St. There were no houses on Campleshon Lane. On the east side of Bishopthorpe Rd were Butcher Terrace, Finsbury St, Terry St and Beresford Terrace.

By 1929 there was much infill in the gaps left in 1907, together with newer streets such as Westwood Terrace (1915) and Jamieson Terrace (1919), again supported by private street works for tarmacking and drainage in 1919. The north side of South Bank Ave was still unbuilt in 1929, as was Campleshon Rd. Knavesmire School, Nunthorpe School, St Chad's Church and the Cameron Walker Homes had appeared, but the land around St Clement's Rectory was still clear of development. The open land between Southlands Rd and South Bank Ave contained allotment gardens and a pond. There used to be a very high wall running all the way around what came to be Nunthorpe School, right down to Bishopthorpe Rd. It featured a plaque, informing people that it was one mile to the station. This wall surrounded allotments, hen runs, pig sties and a large pond, with ducks and very often swans.

Crowd celebrating the coronation of George VI in May 1937, with Southlands Church in the background. (Barbara Weatherley)

There was later inter-war housing development, such as Rectory Gardens, Westwood Terrace and Montague St, and on Albemarle Rd. In 1936 a large estate was built between Southlands Rd and South Bank Ave, known by locals as the 'New Estate', on land formerly part of the grounds of Nunthorpe Court, a large Victorian villa. Later known as the Nunthorpe estate, it was rumoured that stone from York Castle which was being demolished was used to fill in the ground here. The houses are different to the older houses in South

Bank, as they are red-brick two storey semis, boasting bay windows and arched porches, built in a crescent and cul-de-sac estate. It now provides a route for pedestrians and cyclists between the South Bank area and Scarcroft Rd, and onwards to the railway station and shops. There are some bungalows built in 1951 facing the Victorian housing on Philadelphia Terrace, on elevated land, the former gardens of Nunthorpe Hall. There are also a small number of properties built more recently, such as Percy Mews.

A memorable feature of the South Bank area is its alleyways, which still have distinctive stable block paviours. Interestingly it is the area which has kept the most of these in York, and some remain as decorative gutters to many of the asphalt road surfaces.

An important feature of the neighbourhood opened in 2001, the Millennium Bridge across the River Ouse. This is located at the end of Butcher Terrace, a new river crossing which joins the communities of South Bank and Fulford. In 1955 a temporary Army bailey bridge had been erected across the river to facilitate army movement from York Barracks on the Fulford side across to Butcher Terrace and then to the Army Tattoo on the Knavesmire.

Living and shopping 'on the Bank'

This densely populated and thriving area once boasted over 100 shops and businesses, with increasing consumer needs arising from urban growth and the development of a mass market for goods from the end of the 19th century. Typically though these shops were for essentials rather than 'desirable' items. But over the 20th century most of these shops closed, driven out of business by the rise of the supermarket, changing shopping habits and trends and access to personal motor transport. There had been many old corner shops colonising these working class areas, almost all of which have now been converted to residential houses, although a few remain, mainly near the racecourse edge of the area. There are also some working men's clubs and pubs, although the influence of the Revd Argles cast a long shadow over drinking in this area in the early 20th century.

Aerial view of South Bank in York today. Note the clear contrast in housing density between late 19th century/early 20th century housing and later house building, for example the Nunthorpe estate and Rectory Gardens. (Map data © 2019: Google, DigitalGlobe)

Local shops and pubs today

Local shops and pubs today

The corner of South Bank Avenue and Bishopthorpe Rd around 1990, showing Baker and Hudson Computers and George King greengrocer's. (Karen Thompson)

Clark's newsagent on the left hand corner of South Bank Ave and Bishopthorpe Rd, ca 1990. (Karen Thompson)

Oral testimonies recall how during the 1930s shoppers might have relied on running up a credit with a local shop, during hard times. They remember rationing issues during World War II, when purchasing choices were limited, for example a household might only be allowed to buy milk from a certain seller, to economise on fuel, although many traders used a horse and cart. It was not until the 1950s that the flow of goods revived.

There have been moves to introduce larger supermarkets into the area, for example in 1983 there were plans to build a superstore on a site next to Terry's factory, and in modern times there was a plan for a Tesco supermarket on the site of the Winning Post pub. Had these plans succeeded then the competition would have caused further shop closures locally.

Although usually shops were listed under a man's name, evidence from the census reveals that the shopkeeper was sometimes a woman, his wife, and of course shops might be run by a widow. Some were 'house' shops, opening up in the front room of a house, with windows directly on the street. The very first shops, in the north-western terraced streets between Albemarle Rd and Ovington Terrace, opened as soon as the houses were built there from 1881, almost all sited on the eastern corners. These were supplying basic commodities: several grocers (some combining with drapery), a butcher, a fried fish shop, a newsagent briefly, a milkseller, an early post office and an off-licence. Fish and chip shops had started as a treat for men returning from the pub. These shops are now sadly just bricked-up corners, and the only business premises still trading here is the South Bank Social Club. Several did not survive trading past World War I, especially as by 1911 there was increasing competition from the newly opened shops in the terraced streets such as Queen Victoria St and the other end of Albemarle Rd. A few lasted through until the 1960s and 1970s, and one, the off-licence, until the 1990s.

The southern end of Albemarle Rd became a trading focus around 1911, with dairymen, grocers, a draper, butchers, bakers and a post office. Many of these premises have survived, still selling basic convenience commodities: a general store, a butcher and a baker, a hairdresser, together with the betting shop which arrived in the 1970s, taking advantage of the pub and the nearby racecourse, and a barber, who moved recently here from round the corner in Brunswick St.

While there have been small shops in some of the other streets, the main axis along Balmoral Terrace and Queen Victoria St benefited from the opening of the tram service to South Bank in 1913. It led to nearly thirty shops opening here, serving all the hundreds of new South Bank residents. Some of these shops dated from the early years of the century, but others opened later, most trading successfully after the tramline closed in 1935, and lasting for several decades. A large Co-operative grocery and butchery shop had opened in Balmoral Terrace in 1902, rather a two-edged sword, threatening price competition to other traders, but acting as a destination anchor for other traders, in the same way that a post office might attract shoppers to a neighbourhood.

South Bank Adult School in 1904, now St Clement's WMC. (Hugh Murray)

The St Clement's Working Men's Club opened at 3 Queen Victoria St in 1908, and the building now occupied by the Club opened in 1903 as an adult school, with many later uses which must have provided much footfall in the street. As well as grocers, drapers, confectioners, greengrocers, butchers and bakers, there were two fish and chip shops, with some buildings providing services such as a doctor, hairdressers, radio and shoe repairers. In Balmoral Terrace some of the buildings are still business premises and those that have closed only did so from the 1980s onwards. In Queen Victoria St there were three peaks for closures, in the 1950s, the 1970s and the 1990s. The last closure, the fish and chip shop, was quite recent.

Another small group of shops took advantage of the busy junction of Bishopthorpe Rd with South Bank Ave and Butcher Terrace. On the east side, the shops opened around the start of the 20th century, mainly grocers in the early days, but also a chemist from the 1920s. On the opposite side the lodge house on the corner of South Bank Ave was used as a newsagent from the 1920s, but the other corner shops only appeared when the new 1930s Nunthorpe estate was built. They are all still trading, apart from the newsagent, which suffered from the typical fate of newsagents in the last twenty years. These newer shops reflect modern pre-occupations, with kitchen design, veterinary services, as well as hair styling.

Behind this junction Finsbury St near the river was a hotspot for trading, benefiting from traffic along Terry Ave. In this small street eleven of the houses were used for trading at some point, many briefly, closing before World War I, but five lasting longer, closing in the 1960s, 1970s and 1980s. Three were dairymen, most of the others were general shops and grocers.

Trafalgar St was another focus, with ten shops trading out of front rooms mainly. Most closed in the late 1950s and 1960s.

People talking about the shops express their feelings about how the local shops contributed to a sense of community.

'In the 50s and 60s it was quite dramatic really. They were shutting down left right and centre, they couldn't cope with the supermarkets.' (*David Meek*).
'People living here did their shopping locally in those days, they didn't go into town, they did a lot of their shopping at the Co-op. You used to put your order in on a morning, mum used to send me on a Thursday morning with her order, then they used to deliver, horse and cart mostly.' (*Joan Jackman*).

'I think the reason why there were so many grocers was that we didn't have any fridges so you virtually shopped every day. My mum didn't have a fridge when I got married in '62. The scullery was so tiny there was no room for a fridge. Then they brought one out and it just slid under the shelf in the pantry.' *(David Meek).*

'Now…with regard to the passing of all these shops…sadly something was lost, virtually every street had at least one. All in their own way a village pump, a ready-made community centre, somewhere for a chat, not only there but going to and fro. A friendly ear and a comforting shoulder in times of trouble. I was too young to know, but I wonder if people, especially old people, were as lonely as people we constantly hear about now. Here was help and advice free, coupled with good sound common sense, and Yorkshire common sense at that! ' *(Derrick Gray).*

'I sometimes feel rather sad when you see in the papers that someone's been dead for six weeks and nobody's known. Well that didn't happen in those days because they were more neighbourly and they would help one another…when someone died most of the people in the street closed their curtains. And when my mum died my dad said to me, David, go round and tell the neighbours not to close their curtains, because your mother hated it! But she did it you see. People looked out for each other in those days.' *(David Meek).*

There were a number of convenient utilities as well as shops. At a time when many people didn't have a telephone at home, there were telephone boxes at the top of South Bank Ave, at the side of the Post Office on Albemarle Rd, at the end of Balmoral Terrace, and near the Winning Post on Bishopthorpe Rd. These have now all been removed, some quite recently. There was also a police box (a 'Tardis') at the end of Balmoral Terrace, removed in the late 1960s/early 1970s. There were post boxes – the first was in the boundary wall between 91 and 93 Bishopthorpe Rd (near Southlands Chapel). This was later removed and a new GR pillar box positioned at the corner of Southlands Rd and Bishopthorpe Rd around 1937. Other boxes were at the corner of Balmoral Terrace and Bishopthorpe Rd (ER VII from around 1910). The box outside the Post Office in Albemarle Rd was removed in 2005 and eventually replaced on the wall of Fred's Bakery, after much campaigning by Fred Thomas and other residents.

Public conveniences were built in 1907 behind the wall on Albermarle Rd, at a lower level, opposite the bottom of Philadelphia Terrace, reached by a flight of steps. They eventually closed in the early 1960s, when a new toilet block was opened at the end of Knavesmire Rd. There were also two separate plans to build men's and women's toilets at the corner of Balmoral Terrace and Bishopthorpe Rd – first in 1914 and the second in 1934. WWI stopped the first and lack of money stopped the second.

Herbert's grocers, on the corner of Queen Victoria St and Albemarle Rd around the 1920s, with the new trams. (Hugh Murray)

At the beginning of the twentieth century most working people would have walked or used bicycles to move around, although traders might use a horse and cart. However an electric tram service had first opened from Fulford to the city centre in January 1910, then a line from the city centre to Dringhouses, and Haxby Rd and Acomb services. The South Bank Tramway was authorised by a 1912 Light Railways (Extension) Order and built by W. Dobson of Edinburgh at a cost of £15,147. The installation of overhead equipment and cables by the York Corporation Electricity Department began on 25 March 1913 and the line opened from the railway station in July 1913. The South Bank service ran from the station via Nunnery Lane and Bishopthorpe Rd to Queen Victoria St, serving the racecourse as well as Terry's, with a scissors crossover at its terminus outside the Post Office. The long curve of the kerbside at the end of Balmoral Terrace joining Bishopthorpe Rd was built to accommodate the electric trams, avoiding a sharper curve which would have been difficult to negotiate. These were a cheaper means of transport for working people, and meant that people could afford to live further away from their workplaces. In 1918 the South Bank tram started through-running to both Haxby and Fulford, provided by the West Yorkshire Road Car Company who had now taken over the routes from York Corporation.

Bishopthorpe Rd looking south, near Southlands Church, with tramlines, in 1919.

Competition soon developed from 1915 from corporation motor-buses and trolley-buses, powered by electricity from overhead cables. These were run at a loss, subsidised by tramway profits, and by the early 1930s there was competition from private bus companies, which were able to extend their routes beyond the reach of the tramlines. Eventually in 1935 the trams and trolley buses were withdrawn. A replacement omnibus service no. 4 started to run between South Bank and Fulford.

'My sister was born at our gran's in Albemarle Rd in 1930. They had to stop the trams at the bottom end as the noise was bringing our Mum round from the ether.' *(Jenny Garbutt).*

'The bus terminus was outside the Knavesmire pub, having done a reversing manoeuvre into Knavesmire Crescent. The tramlines stopped outside the old Post Office.' *(John Daniel).*

'I remember the tramlines being pulled up in 1934. Lads would gather up the 'tar logs' from the tramlines and they would go on people's fires.' *(Barbara Weatherley).*

Derrick Gray recorded the popular street games and pastimes which young residents used to occupy their time with 'on the Bank':

'Four wheels and a board was always popular with boys. For this, you needed four pram wheels and a plank of wood. The wheels were attached to the board using lashings of either rope or wire, the four holes required for this were made using a red hot poker…The front axle was on a pivot, and a length of rope was tied to each end of the axle for the steering gear, then away to the nearest slope. The road known as 'Sleepers ' was the best, then there was South Bank Ave, or the slope from the Ave into Brunswick St. There were no houses on one side of Sleepers (I still call the slope up from Brunswick Street to Ovington Terrace and South Bank Ave, Sleepers, because that is precisely what was there in those days…railway sleepers). There were very few cars. Pedestrians didn't count. If you didn't get them coming down, you did your best on the way back up!
'Stilt walking as a pastime went on for a week or two after every Race Meeting. We used the 2 by 1 inch pieces of timber the bookies left behind from their stands.
'Swapping ciggies [cigarette cards] was almost a year-round occupation, involving not only boys but fathers as well. A full set was usually fifty, and they could be footballers, cricketers, racehorses, ships, trains, you name it. In my early days at work as a boy, older men went round at break time saying 'Hey, my lad wants number 24 or 32 for a full set of either Park Drive or Woodbines'. Ciggie cards were also used in games. One I call to mind was propping them up against a wall and flicking another card at them, ducks and drakes style. If you knocked one down it was yours. If you missed you lost yours. An often-tried scheme, which usually failed, was to try to persuade your dad to change his brand of cigarettes because you didn't like the cards his normal brand were offering! Today, these same cards, in albums, are bringing hundreds of pounds at auctions.'

The area starts to develop

The 1892 Ordnance Survey map shows two large houses, Nunthorpe Court and Nunthorpe Hall, on the north western edge of South Bank, and a small group of large houses much further south, alongside the river. There are two other imposing buildings, the new Southlands Wesleyan Methodist Chapel on the corner of Southlands Rd, and St Clement's Rectory, standing alone in the fields to the south. On Southlands Terrace there was a row of newly built imposing houses, but the only part of South Bank otherwise developed for worker housing at the time was the north west corner, with four small terraced streets built around 1881: Adelaide St, Argyle St, Windsor St and the south side of Philadelphia Terrace. These were bounded by Ovington Road to the east, and Albemarle Terrace to the west. William Chapman, later known as 'Count de Burgh', was behind quite a few of these new housing developments.

In 1890 a press report explained that 'South Bank' referred to 'several streets and terraces on the high ground between the Knavesmire and Bishopthorpe, where quite a village of people find themselves situate with what they denounce…as inadequate approaches, as an "Avenue" to Bishopthorpe Rd, in which lamps are placed that are never lit.' The report arose from a sudden event, the collapse of around 50–60 yards of wall overlooking the Knavesmire, supposedly due to pressure from the newly built houses.

At this time houses here were described surprisingly as at 'The Mount', meaning an area rather than the street of that name today. What sort of people were moving into these newly-built small terraced streets? The 1881 census lists skilled artisans and their families – machinists, engine fitters, railway clerks, porters and guards, carriage builders, boilermakers, blacksmiths, railway labourers. These would have had a secure wage from the new railway employers.

As soon as these streets began to fill with people then shops started to open to supply them with necessities, and these were the first wave of shops in our area. The first was in 1881, a grocer William Ernest on the corner of Windsor St, who lasted around twelve years there. By 1895 there were several corner shops such as off-licences, butchers and provision grocers. A shop on the corner of Philadelphia Terrace and

Albemarle Terrace was a grocer, post, money order office and savings bank in 1895. Today none of these shops remain, only the South Bank Social Club is still trading.

Shop on the corner of Albermarle Terrace and Philadelphia Terrace, around 1900. (Hugh Murray)

The following lists traders who were known to be in business from the address described. Evidence in York directories is sometimes unclear, as dates cannot be strictly relied upon. Often they related to the year before the date of publication, and it is also sometimes unclear if a person was in business at an address, as opposed to a private resident. It might be a man listed whose wife was the trader. Sometimes a trader had retired but was still at the address. Educated guesses have been made about the length of trading. Once the last trader had closed, these premises were converted into private housing, leaving shadows in the bricks as the only evidence.

Records show that William Chapman (later known as De Burgh) applied for planning permission for 38 houses in Argyle St in 1880, 12 houses in 'Windsor Terrace' in 1881, 16 houses in Philadelphia Terrace in 1882, and more ambitiously 39 houses in Albemarle Terrace in 1881/2. This wasn't his only area of interest, as he was also involved in developments in other areas, such as Leeman Road and Hull Road.

No. 1 Adelaide St

There was a grocer here at the south-east corner of the street from around 1881. John Aitchison Jackson was working as a machinist and living with his wife and three sons at this address in that year, but was soon in business as a grocer, a provision dealer with an 'off' beer licence. This lasted until around 1898, when one of his sons, John Whitaker Jackson, took over. He was still listed there in the early 1920s, when the shop and house was recorded as 4 Ovington Terrace. It is not clear if he was trading in the 1920s and early 1930s, although in 1929 he was recorded as running an off-licence next door at no 3, and then Theresa Cullabine similarly in 1935.

George Chapman ran an off-licence at this address for a long time, from around 1936 until 1974. From 1939–1971 he was also recorded as living at 4 Ovington Terrace. For the last ten years of his shop he seems to have gone rather up-market, as he described himself as a wine merchant. Eventually in 1975 the shop became Daniel's off-licence, then Day's, Brown's, and the Corner Cask, before finally closing down in 1994.

No. 27 Adelaide St

On the south west corner, next to the back alleyway, George Everitt traded as a butcher in a shop here. In the 1880s he cleaned out his shop every Saturday night so that it could be used as a Sunday School on Sunday mornings. This was so successful that it eventually moved into two houses in a neighbouring street, and services for adults began to be held there.

At the same time a large Methodist church inside the city walls was seeking to respond to the growing population just outside the walls, and Everitt's Sunday school work, with money and personnel made available by the big church, resulted in the opening of Southlands Methodist Church in 1887. This took advantage of a prominent site previously occupied by a windmill at the top of the hill in Bishopthorpe Rd.

George did appear in the newspaper one year, when he was involved in a court case in April 1895. He'd been summoned to appear before the Eastern Ainsty Petty Sessions, for causing two of his pigs to be moved out of the West Riding, an infected area at the time. An apprentice had been stopped on Bishopthorpe Rd driving a cart with two 'store pigs', bringing them back from Bishopthorpe, where he'd been raising them. He claimed that he was not aware that he needed a licence to move the pigs, but was fined 1s plus costs. Everitt seems to have moved around the corner to 1 Albemarle Rd around that time, to bigger premises.

In 1895 the shop at no.27 was a grocer, but importantly also a post office and savings bank, run by Dennis Frederick. Later shopkeepers were Pearson Greenwood (1897). Mr Cross (1898), John William Gooch and Emma Gooch (1901–5), Nelly Thomlinson (1909) and Percy Wood (1913). The positioning of this shop at the bottom end of the terrace, rather than the more prominent top end, together with the advent of war, seem to have hindered trading opportunities, and the house has been a private residence since that period.

No. 28 Adelaide St
On the opposite corner of Adelaide St, again next to the back alleyway, there was a short appearance of a provision shop, run by Martha Barff for around ten years from 1891. She was replaced briefly by John Brummitt in 1905.

No. 19 Argyle St
The house and shop here were advertised to let in 1881, as 'the owners were leaving town'. It was a fried fish shop in 1901 and then a number of traders are recorded: Samuel Parker (1905–1909), Arthur Dalby (1911), Thomas Kirby (1913). From the 1920s there was Charles Ingram (1925–1932), A R Malarky (1935–1938), H W Bell (1949–50), and the long-lasting H Sturdy (1951–1970). Later came Smith's, Giovanni's, then Eden's, with the shop finally closing in 1975. It still however retains its oblique corner shop appearance today.

'When Smith's had it there was also a wet fish outlet at the back.' *(Keith Watson).*

'In those days fish and chips was a cheap meal, not like now. We used to have fish and chips most often on a Friday.' *(David Meek).*

No. 21 Argyle St and Nos. 22–25 Argyle St South Bank WMC
The Club's address is now 12 Ovington Terrace (see page 29).

Windsor St

In 1881 a new Wesleyan mission room was opened at 5 Windsor St, needed because of a rapidly increasing population. It included a large upper room accommodating 80 persons and two classrooms. This was occasionally used for other purposes, as in 1899 a meeting was held there to protest against a proposal from John J. Hunt Ltd for a new public house, led by Rev Argles and Robert Kay. It was recorded that "In the opinion of this meeting the granting of further facilities for the sale of intoxicating liquors upon the South Bank estate is unnecessary and undesirable". There wasn't a huge turnout for this, records show that there were only 20 people there because of rain on that day and only 8 voted.

Lonsdale's grocery and drapery shop on the corner of Windsor St and Ovington Terrace, with Ernest Algernon Lonsdale and Mary Lonsdale. (Marion Goodrick)

No. 1 Windsor St

The first shop in South Bank opened here in 1881, when William Ernest was listed as a grocer from 1881 to 1893, starting as soon as the street was built. By 1894 a trader, possibly Ernest, was advertising a 'rulley and harness' here for sale (a rulley was a kind of lorry used for street deliveries). From 1895–1898 it was James Lonsdale, grocer and draper, who had moved from the bottom end of the street at no 15, where he had been trading from 1889. In 1900 no 1 was Henry Sharp grocer and draper, but Mary Anne Lonsdale took over again in 1901, lasting until the 1940s, when it was Ernest Algernon Lonsdale, who ran the shop until around 1960. By 1961 it was J Watson shopkeeper, but it is not clear how long he stayed in business. (See also 8 Ovington Terrace). As well as drapery Mary also ran her dressmaking business from 1 Windsor Street, using the front room as a waiting room and fitting room. The two properties were joined at the back of the shop with a connecting door.

No. 15 Windsor St
This was another early shop, with grocer and draper James Lonsdale here from 1889, until he moved up to no. 1 at the top end of the street in 1895, when Harry Sturdy became shopkeeper here, listed in directories until 1902, although Emma Sturdy was in the census as shopkeeper in 1901. In 1905 it was Albert Ernest Bean, until at least 1913, although Alice Bean also had a listing in 1913.

It later became a boot and shoe repairer, first Reginald Farmery (who seems to have moved to Brunswick St by the 1930s), then Mr Bean, until around 1935.

No. 23 Windsor St
This was briefly a newsagents around 1911–1913, Frederick Shuttleworth, but the Shuttleworth's moved their business to no 2 South Bank Ave from 1921, lasting there until the death of his wife Hannah in 1937.

No. 39 Albemarle Rd (previously no. 1)
There was a shop on the corner of Philadelphia Terrace, originally no 1 but now no. 39. In 1892 a house and shop was advertised to let in Philadelphia Terrace, suitable for a grocer or draper, fixtures at a valuation, almost certainly this one. It was grocer John Henry Pilmoor in 1893 until 1896, then in 1897 it became a butcher, George Everitt, until at least 1913. Much later, in the 1960s and early 1970s it was Colette, ladies' hairdresser, finally closing in 1974.

Ovington Terrace (previously Ovington Road)

In 1881 there was a row of five large terraced houses, at the top of what was to be South Bank Ave, built for Nunthorpe Hall estate workers, the original Ovington Terrace. Other smaller houses were constructed to the north, often shops sharing addresses between Ovington Terrace and its adjoining streets.

In 1900 it was reported that an open air meeting was held outside the Mission Room in Ovington Terrace, for a York City by-election.

'Starting with Ovington Terrace, commencing with the back lane. From the top, when I was a boy, you were faced with a large gate, through which was a slaughterhouse. Mr. Knowles, the dairyman from Albemarle Road, did the slaughtering for Mr. Boyes (later Mrs. Boyes) and Mr. Everitt, Philadelphia Terrace butchers. Just behind this, with access to Hubert Street, was a rather large garage. A well-known South Bank character called Bill Exelby kept a charabanc in it, replaced later with taxis, and later still an overnight garage for local people, now two houses.' *(Derrick Gray).*

'This garage was also where Charles Burgess of Albermarle Road, dairyman, kept his milk delivery van around the 1960s.' *(Keith Watson).*

No. 1 Ovington Terrace
This was at the northern end of Ovington Terrace, with William Exelby, farmer and milkseller, here in 1901 and again in 1911, when his son William Meek Exelby was another milk dealer. But subsequently this address disappears from listings, and the Exelby family seem to have moved to a larger house at the southern end, at no. 22 for a long period. William Exelby played a key role in the establishment of the South Bank Working Men's Club, as a continuous member for 53 years.

No. 4 Ovington Terrace
No. 4 was linked to no. 1 Adelaide St, as John Whitaker Jackson's off-licence was recorded at the latter from around 1890, and he was living at 4 Ovington Terrace in the 1920s. Again George Chapman was listed as living at no. 4, from 1939–1971, while running an off-licence at no. 1 Adelaide St from around 1936 to 1974. It later became Daniel's off-licence, then Day's, and Brown's. It was the Corner Cask in the 1980s and finally closed in 1994, converted into a house.

No. 5 Ovington Terrace

This was the original site of the South Bank Working Men's Club, which had opened there in 1881. With as many as 400 to 500 people living in the vicinity, the vicar of St Mary's Bishophill had rented a house and was providing rooms here for reading, smoking and games.

No. 8 Ovington Terrace

This corner shop was linked to 1 Windsor St, with the long-standing grocers Lonsdale's. It was listed here from 1939, and up to 1957. Later it was Poole's, Machen's, McNichol's and Wilton's. It appeared to close around 1973.

South Bank Social Club

The club is now at 12 Ovington Terrace.

South Bank Social Club today. (Susan Major)

The inaugural meeting of South Bank Working Men's Club was held at Lawrence Street Working Men's Club in 1899, which led to the opening of the club in six cottages in Argyle St in November 1899. Four were converted into a large clubroom, one was for the steward and the other sublet. Their Cricket Club and an Angling Association was founded in 1900. L. P. Codona was the club steward in 1900 at no. 21, and James Chapman was the club secretary at no. 22. In 1909 an adjoining cottage was demolished so that the main room of the Club could be extended, and in 1919 the club became the property of its members. It changed to the current address in 1953. In 1963 a seventh house was bought in Argyle Street so the sixth house was demolished to further extend the main room. The building previously included a room for members' wives, who were allowed in from 1950. In 1990 the Club was refurbished at a cost of £55,000.

In a new development Young Thugs was established at the Club in 2016 as a community platform for the York music scene, including artist management, recording studio and unusual events. They combine cutting edge digital recording with classic analogue equipment. Their music has been heard on national radio stations around the world and used in the TV and film industry. Young Thugs are based upstairs, in the old committee and treasurer's rooms.

'In the 1990s the Club had about 800 members, plus 100 lady members. Many activities took place, including outdoor bowls, two teams of indoor bowlers, darts and 'fives and threes' teams, snooker, two football teams, two quiz teams and a walking section. Surprisingly it also had a rifle range, and an extensive library.

'When I joined the Club as a young man, the library was the attraction. Thursday night was library night, so depending on finances, bearing in mind pay-day was Friday, I went to the Club for either a pint and change of books or just the latter. The advent of TV killed the library off, unfortunately. There was dancing on Saturday nights to live music, and bingo sessions, and every Sunday night there was live entertainment. Some show business celebrities have performed in the Club over the years: Paul Daniels, Paul Shane (*Hi-Di-Hi*), Bernie Clifton and Charlie Williams, who performed after he became a star on TV, for his original fee of £30.

'It was at that social club that it all began for Ovington, probably in 1928… the younger players at South Bank Cricket Club weren't getting a game, so they formed their own team, taking their name from the terrace South Bank's club house stands on. Nearly 90 years on, South Bank CC has long gone, while Ovington prospers, with three senior teams, an evening-league team, and half a dozen junior teams.' (*Derrick Gray*).

South Bank Workmen's Club Cricket Club, August 1925.

South Bank AFC 1916–17. (Geoff Shearsmith)

Southlands Chapel, opened 1887. (Hugh Murray)

Southlands Methodist Church

By the 1880s the local population was growing fast, and a Methodist chapel was needed outside of the city walls, to offer educational opportunities for the working class, children and young adults alike in the South Bank area. Although generally the leading people in the York chapels were middle class, many of the congregation were shopkeepers, traders and skilled artisans, and Wesleyan chapels were more working class than other non-conformist chapels.

The church began as a Sunday school, held in George Everitt's butcher's shop at the bottom of Adelaide St. He cleaned out the shop on a Saturday night ready for Sunday morning and this venture was so successful it soon transferred to a new Wesleyan mission room in 1885 at 5 Windsor St, with a large upper room accommodating 80 persons and two classrooms.

The move to build a new church was supported by several local businessmen and by a large church inside the city walls. Charles Bell, a specialist in Wesleyan Methodist chapels had designed more than

60 churches around the country, and now designed the new chapel for South Bank. It provided for a congregation of 750 in the main church which had a balcony, three meeting rooms and a Sunday school block with 15 classrooms. Southlands Wesleyan Chapel opened on 13 October 1887, on a site in Southlands Rd previously occupied by the Nun Windmill and later by a quarry.

The move of the locomotive works from York to Darlington in 1905 was reported to have hit the church badly. But after the war in 1920 an additional single-storey building with two large rooms was built on land adjoining the church, providing social facilities for young men unable to find work after returning from service in the Great War. This was called the Thanksgiving Hall and also provided facilities for the church's Young Men's Association and other activities. In more recent years the Hall was used by Terry Berry for his photography business.

Southlands has responded in many ways to community needs, for example providing leisure facilities for soldiers during two world wars, and providing shelter and help for refugees from Belgium during the Great War and from Hungary in the mid-1950s. It now has a programme of youth and children's work and, more recently, has become a hub for the arts with 18 artists working out of 11 art studios established on the former balcony of the church and on the gallery in the Community Centre, formerly the Sunday school block.

In addition Seek Art School offers art courses, rooms on the premises are hired out to community groups, including choirs, theatre groups, a jazz dance group, a Brazilian martial arts group, Song Box (a music group for toddlers), and a community café.

In 1971 the Church was renovated at a cost of £9,000, with pews removed. Further work was carried out in the Millennium Year and again in 2019, when the art studios were established. After almost 100 years the Thanksgiving Hall was demolished in 2016.

Nunthorpe Court

The building upon which Millthorpe School is based was formerly Nunthorpe Court, a mansion built in 1856, designed by York's Atkinson brothers, the firm founded by John Carr. Its estate of over

Nunthorpe Court, built in 1856.

33 acres, extended to Bishopthorpe Rd. There was a driveway on Nunthorpe Ave and a lodge at the current junction of Bishopthorpe Rd and Southlands Rd, with a driveway in from the east. The lodge was demolished in 1885, making way for the new Methodist Chapel. This approach to the house was closed in 1937, with the site being developed for eight houses at the western end of Southlands Rd.

In the early days it was known as Nunthorpe Grove, and George Wilson JP lived here from 1861 to 1879, and then, briefly, Major Charles Balacaw. From 1886 for over 30 years it was home to Colonel Richard Frederick Meysey-Thompson (1847–1926) and his wife Charlotte. It was a large estate, in 1888 he advertised around 24 acres as summer 'eatage', 'well-watered and fences good'. Meysey-Thompson was a soldier from a military family. He served in the Rifle Brigade, on active duty from 1866, and fought in the second phase of the Ashanti conflict (modern day Ghana) during 1873 and 1874. He retired from the army in 1884, due to malaria. In 1889 he was re-appointed Lt Col of the 4th Battalion Prince of Wales's Own (West Yorkshire Regiment), and the honorary rank of Colonel was conferred in 1890. Richard was a keen owner and trainer of horses, and his wife Charlotte, who died in 1935, was a nationally renowned horsewoman.

The Meysey-Thompsons were living at Nunthorpe Court during World War I and were involved in various tribunal cases involving staff and military service. The building suffered war damage, set on fire by three bombs hitting the roof and chimney stacks, and impassable chasms were left in the driveway.

Nunthorpe Court eventually became the home of Richard's son, Sir Algar De Clifford Charles Meysey-Thompson, who sold the house in 1920 to York Corporation, along with 11 acres of land, for £10,750, a relatively low amount at the time. Algar then moved to live in the lodge at the Nunthorpe Ave entrance, where he died aged 82 in 1967. Approximately 22 acres of land from the old estate were sold in 1935 to Harry and Louise Williamson from Heworth Green, and the Nunthorpe estate was developed, with many houses in Nunthorpe Grove and Nunthorpe Crescent selling for £475.

The Council opened Nunthorpe Court Secondary School for Boys in 1920, much needed because of a great demand for secondary education for boys at this time, with the overcrowding at Archbishop Holgate's School. At that time however less than 5% of boys in primary education in York went on to secondary education. When it opened the school had 49 boys, of whom 27 were fee-paying.

The school grew quickly. In 1927 a north-west wing was added as a hall/gymnasium, with another new hall and quadrangle in 1937. The Corporation also bought Mill Mount House for £8,000 for use as a girls' school. The two schools could each accommodate 200 pupils.

The start of the autumn term in 1939 was delayed because of the need to strengthen the cellars for air raid shelters. In the 1942 Baedeker air raid on York most of the windows at the front of the old building were smashed, and a member of staff was killed. The kitchen was damaged by the falling engine of a Halifax bomber which exploded in mid-air.

The 1944 Education Act led to a change from secondary school for boys to boys' grammar school, and in 1950 it was renamed Nunthorpe Grammar School. There were further additions: a new block of classrooms in 1959, a sixth form block in 1974 and a sports hall in 1984. In 1985, as York went comprehensive, Nunthorpe and Mill Mount schools merged to become Millthorpe School, with pupils from other York schools joining. The school is now part of the South Bank Academy Trust.

Kentmere House and 1 Telford Terrace
Now Kentmere Art Gallery and offices for MCA Funding for Churches

Kentmere House, on the corner of Scarcroft Hill and Telford Terrace, was the home of the Primitive Methodist Chapel Aid Association (PMCAA). This was set up in 1890 by Sir William Pickles Hartley of Hartley's Jam, to raise money for loan to debt-ridden chapels on the cheapest terms. At this time there was a boom in chapel-building and the Primitive Methodists had debts of over £1 million. York was chosen as its base because of railway links with Northern towns, where its directors, all businessmen, lived. It was based first at 63 Bishopthorpe Rd, but later moved to Telford Terrace in January 1900. The house had been built in 1898 and there is still an inscribed stone to that effect built into the front of the house.

Kentmere House today. (Susan Major)

Kentmere House accommodated its Secretary, with a separate wing for the housekeeper and nursery, with offices and boardroom next door, and a connecting door. There was a small strong room with two-foot thick walls, where they kept the chapel deeds while loans were outstanding. This was demolished in the late 1990s (once deeds had been computerised by the Land Registry) to provide additional office space. The entire property was later sold in 1983, PMCAA retaining a lease on the office area. The lease has been renewed and PMCAA, now operating as MCA Funding for Churches, is still at 1 Telford Terrace and now supports churches of all denominations.

For four years prior to 1991 the house was occupied by Madeleine Evans, a homeopath and since 1991 the house has become the Kentmere House Art Gallery, owned by Ann and David Petherick, chosen because of its large rooms with high ceilings and a spacious staircase – perfect for displaying original art. Ann's previous gallery was at Grape Lane.

Nunthorpe Hall

Nunthorpe Hall was demolished over 40 years ago, thus many will not know of it or perhaps confuse it with Nunthorpe Court, which still stands. It was designed and built in 1866/7 by local architect Herbert Fippard, for mining engineer Henry Johnson McCulloch. Plans called it 'South Bank House' or 'Captain McCulloch's Mansion'. The Hall was on an elevated position overlooking the little Knavesmire, reached from a long driveway off Bishopthorpe Rd.

McCulloch was a prominent York citizen with a reputation for commercial interests, following employment by the North Eastern Railway. He was involved with philanthropic movements, a founder of Elmfield College, and a guarantor of the York Exhibition of 1886. He was prominent in the Primitive Methodist Church and a Liberal councillor for Micklegate ward in the 1860s. However following unsuccessful speculation he had to sell the mansion soon after and left York in 1868. But his fortunes revived and he became consulting engineer to the Admiralty.

The sale particulars describe 'a handsome and commodious residence… overlooking Knavesmire, replete with every modern accessory of reception, domestic and culinary arrangement, together with Garden and Stable requirement'. Plans included provision for a game larder, a meat larder and a china closet at the rear of the ground floor behind the entrance hall. The gardens extended down to Albemarle Rd and bordered the entire length of Philadelphia Terrace.

Nunthorpe Hall. (Hugh Murray)

The carriage drive to Bishopthorpe Rd had a lodge and 'tasteful' entrance gates, opening into an avenue of chestnut, lime and sycamore trees, around 600 yards long. This road was originally described in maps as The Avenue, but when houses were built on it in the early 1900s it was renamed South Bank Avenue.

Nunthorpe Hall was sold at auction in 1870 to Mr J A Reim of Sunderland, for £6,200. Subsequently the Armitage family were there in the 1870s, and Isaac Wilson in 1879. But there is some surprising evidence from 1881 and 1885 that local property speculator William Chapman, the famous 'Count de Burgh' was living there in that period, and a memorial to him at St Chad's Church from 1926 refers to him as being 'late of Nunthorpe Hall'.

A family of wealthy industrialists, the Lycett-Green's, moved to York in 1888 to live at Nunthorpe Hall. Their fortunes had been made by Edward Green, who had bought the invention of a successful fuel economiser from a Leeds engineer in 1843, and used his business acumen to make a fortune from it, together with his son, Edward Lycett-Green, who became the 1st baronet. The latter became a good friend of King Edward, as their Norfolk estates were alongside each other. His son, Edward, the 2nd Bt and wife Ethel Lycett-Green were involved in the famous baccarat scandal at Tranby Croft, near Hull, in 1890, involving the Prince of Wales.

Edward and Ethel were living at 2 Mount Villas in 1891, on the Mount, and a little later at Knavesmire Lodge, 304 Tadcaster Rd, and then Ashfield in Dringhouses. Sir Edward's second son Frank Green, the well-known York industrialist and property developer, lived at the Treasurer's House in York. The 1st Baronet lived at Nunthorpe Hall until the death of his wife in 1902, and then moved to be with Frank, and died in 1923. In 1911 the census listed 15 servants at the Hall, including a number of grooms, but no householder.

VAD nurses at Nunthorpe Hall during World War I. (Mike Pollard)

During World War I Nunthorpe Hall was lent to the Red Cross by Sir Edward as Nunthorpe Hall York Auxiliary VAD Military Hospital, to receive men injured in the Battle of Loos in 1915. It had 50 beds at first, increasing to 76 beds, and was managed by Sir Edward's daughter-in-law Ethel Lycett-Green. Even there the men were not safe, as on the night of 2/3 May 1916 two Zeppelin bombs set fire to the upper house and four fell in the garden, resulting in considerable damage and the evacuation of the hospital. All patients survived as they were on ground floor.

Ethel Lycett-Green was the Commandant, assisted by a female Quartermaster. Trained staff included a matron, three sisters and two Medical Officers, Dr Armytage, and Dr. Louise Fraser – a pioneer of women's medicine who had launched a public appeal to establish York's first maternity home. There were in addition 24 VADs (Voluntary Aid Detachment nurses), two cooks and two charwomen. VADs carried out duties that were less technical, but no less important, than trained nurses. By the time the hospital closed in April 1919, the staff had treated a total of 915 patients, and Mrs. Lycett-Green received an OBE award for her wartime work there.

The Hall was eventually sold to John Hetherton in 1921 and converted into 16 flats. It was demolished in 1977 and Coggan Close built on the area. A small lodge, built in the 1930s, still remains at the entrance to Coggan Close, where it adjoins Millthorpe School at Ovington Terrace.

Further housing development

Developer William Chapman began to apply for planning permission for streets of houses under his assumed name, De Burgh, after 1891, and between 1897 and 1913 had schemes for houses in many local streets: 75 cottages in Kensington St (1899), 20 houses in Westwood Terrace (1900), 8 houses in Brunswick Rd (1903), 10 cottages in South Bank Ave (1905), 6 cottages in Curzon Terrace (1905), 3 houses in Albemarle Rd (1907), 4 houses in Knavesmire Cres (1910), a shop in Albemarle Rd (1910), and 12 cottages and a house in Montague St (1911/1913).

Another local builder, John Thomas Wood was heavily involved with schemes too: 26 cottages in Finsbury Terrace (1899), 4 houses in Beresford Terrace (1899), 12 houses and cottages in Finsbury Terrace (1910/3), and 4 cottages in Butcher Terrace (1903).

After 1900 a large number of streets with densely packed terraces of housing were built and named with a Victorian theme. More shops opened. These were usually on street corners, with a doorway cut into the corner at an angle, where they might guarantee better business. But several shops were created in the middle of a terrace, opening into the front room of a house.

There were informal traders too. Derrick Gray remembered a local character called 'Watercress Charlie', who lived in Knavesmire Woods, in a primitive home with a watercress bed. He picked this and sold it 'round the Bank'.

'In later years there were other mobile businesses in addition to milk deliveries – I remember a mobile greengrocer and fruiterer who used to travel around the local streets, called Fred Lofthouse, whose van was garaged in premises off Dalton Terrace.' *(Keith Watson)*.

The tram service between the city centre and Queen Victoria St may have helped traders concentrate in this street, particularly towards the west end, nearer the Knavesmire. A secondary area was Finsbury St, between Bishopthorpe Rd and the river. These often sold basic items, such as grocers, butchers, greengrocers, newsagents, confectioners and drapers. Milk and coal dealers featured frequently.

The following directory lists shop and business premises, starting with Albemarle Rd, a focus for trading at the west side of South Bank. It can be difficult to assess the nature of business roles listed in directories, as often a man would be listed as the shopkeeper, whereas the census might record that he was working on the railway or in the chocolate factory, and it was his wife who was running the business.

Albemarle Rd

In 1853 a substantial wall was built alongside Micklegate Stray as part of the later Nunthorpe Hall estate. By 1889 the map of York shows Albemarle Terrace as an early road, developed by William Chapman (later De Burgh) around 1882. It extended south from no.1 on the corner of Philadelphia Terrace, down towards the back alleyway of Argyle St. At one point this was referred to as South Bank Rd. Keith Watson noted that his dad remembered a well at the bottom of Philadelphia Terrace on the opposite side to the old shop, part of the old Nunthorpe Hall Estate, and even today the boundary wall of the current corner building is cut off at an angle.

The houses at nos. 1–34 Albermarle Terrace appear in the 1891 census, and then in 1901, Albermarle Rd is listed, with nos. 35–55, followed by

Albemarle Rd from the Mount, before it was widened in 1922. The area was called South Mount Terrace at the time. The house is now Mount Royale Hotel.

even nos. 36–54, and then the Post Office. By 1911 these addresses had been combined as nos. 1–166 Albemarle Rd, but spelling of the road varies historically between Albemarle and Albermarle. In 1922 it was widened near the junction with The Mount and the whole re-named Albemarle Rd to match the existing road at the South Bank end.

A well-known local family, the Bousfields, lived at the fine-looking West House on Albemarle Road, built in the 1890s and overlooking the Knavesmire.

Matthew, standing at the top of the steps on the photograph was the head of the family and the original source of the family's income. He lived in Leeds but had founded the family business, Bar Works in Micklegate, in the 1860s, a whitesmith's and bell hangers, later diversifying with other metal goods. He passed the business on to his son John in 1886, and John and his family lived at West House from the late 1890s until around 1913. John was a keen cyclist and cycle maker. The Bar Ironworks business later moved to Cromwell Rd. His wife Sarah Bousfield was a milliner, with a shop in Micklegate.

The family car was probably a 30-horsepower Beeston Humber. New, it cost over £560 in 1907. At this time there were fewer than twelve

The Bousfield family, at Albe(r)marle Rd around 1907. (YAYAS)

individuals licensed to drive in the South Bank, Knavesmire and Clementhorpe area, so this car was something of an expensive novelty.

In 1906 it was found necessary to open a gentlemen's public convenience opposite the junction with Philadelphia Terrace, possibly associated with pedestrian traffic from the races here. This closed in 1961, to be replaced by new conveniences on Knavesmire Rd in the old Royal Observer Corps building.

A purpose-built building on Knavesmire Rd had opened in 1942 for the Royal Observer Corps York 10 Group, vacated in 1961 when the Group moved to an underground HQ at Shelley House in Holgate. Sadly it has now been demolished. A WWll air raid shelter on Albemarle Rd dates from around 1939, one of very few remaining. It is now used as a cricket pavilion and changing room, still serving the local community.

In 1983 British Telecom moved the public telephone box from outside the Post Office to Campleshon Rd. In 2000 Knavesmire Rd was closed, due to the highest floods for 400 years, and pleasure boats were used for trips across the Knavesmire.

Royal Observer Corps York 10 during World War II. (Geoff Shearsmith)

A number of the old shops on this road have lasted, helped by their proximity to the racecourse and to the Knavesmire public house.

No. 74 Albemarle Rd
Currently Tranquil Hair and Beauty

This was built in 1908 as a private house, with a proviso (typical in this area) that it should not be used to sell intoxicating liquor either in club or shop, or as a fried fish shop. The conveyance from 1908 mentions John Cooper de Burgh, William Chapman de Burgh's son.

In the 1930s it housed a grocer's shop over a long period, Walter Willson Ltd, sharing the premises with W J Chippendale, newsagent. Willson's stayed here until the 1970s. After the grocers left there was a range of traders: Knavesmire Television, Hunters, The Shed Car Accessories, before it embarked on housing personal services. In the 1980s it was Harrison-Raw Hair Stylists (see also Queen Victoria St), and then Ebony Hair and Nail Studio. There was also chiropody, first Christine's Chiropodist, then Zena Blackwell (house calls only). Colette Cross opened Tranquil Hair and Beauty in 2008, offering a wide selection of hair, beauty and nail treatments.

Albemarle Rd near end of Brunswick St, around 1910. (Keith Watson)

No. 120 Albemarle Rd

Charles Alfred Burgess was a long-standing dairyman here, one of several in the area. He was listed in 1927, but it is not clear when he was officially trading, as the first record was in 1931. He closed in 1963. In 1977 plans were approved for the building of five garages and two new houses at the top of Hubert Street, on the former Burgess Dairy site.

'Our milkman was called Burgess...and he used to deliver in jugs. You put your jug on doorstep, just fancy open like that, well they had a thing on top of it, then we got bottles.' *(Joan Jackman)*.

No. 129 Albemarle Rd (previously no. 57)
Currently D & K Stores, general store and off licence

This shop, on the northern corner of Brunswick Street, has over 100 years of trading. It was originally a grocer around 1905, and listed as a fruiterer in 1911, Arthur Rose, changing to Albert Sykes in 1922, then George Sykes from around 1953 until 1973. It became a grocer again, Todd's, in 1974, and then went through a number of trades, GS Upholstery, Royce Harmer Art Studio, the Food Chain, and Bubbles in the 1990s, followed by D & K Stores. Harish and Bijal Patel have now absorbed the former barber's shop round the corner into their building and have refurbished the grocer's shop, a welcome resource in this densely built-up area.

No. 131 Albemarle Rd (previously no. 59)
On the opposite corner of Brunswick St, with some confusion between listings as 120 Brunswick St, and 131 Albemarle Rd, there was a house and shop in 1901, the latter belonging to Susan Rose, a fancy draper from 1901 to 1905, then in 1913 a draper and milliner, Miss Elizabeth Gibson. In the 1920s the name changed to R. Lemmon, who was previously a newsagent in Queen Victoria St, possibly listed as a male partner of the milliner.

Brunswick St around 1905, with grocer Arthur Rose on the left and draper Susan Rose on the right. We have been unable to find a family connection. (John Pollard)

By 1927 it had changed to Irwin Richard Brown, baker and confectioner, and remained Brown's Bakery until the early 1950s, when it became Parkinson's Bakery, with Ellen Parkinson in charge. By 1967 it was Haxby's, and then Pavlo's Bakery (supplier only). In the 1980s it became Fred's Bakery, who subsequently moved around to the corner of Albemarle Rd and Queen Victoria St. This shop closed in 1994.

No. 133 Albemarle Rd (previously no. 61)
Currently Fred's Bakery.

This shop was on the corner of Queen Victoria St and Albemarle Rd. In the 1920s and 1930s Ebor Fireworks was listed after no.117 Queen Victoria St, where Ernest Sowray lived. During the war it was W. Wright & Sons (York) Ltd pork butchers, with the Sowray family living there until at least 1975. It was later used as a store place for a plumber, who sold it to Fred Thomas and then became Fred's Wholesale Bakery in 1995, now a retail bakery for many years, Fred's Home Bakery, with another shop in Bishopthorpe.

Fred Thomas has been a well-known South Bank baker for 38 years, the longest serving trader in our area. He has been a baker since he left school, coming from a family of ten, and recalls being sent to the baker as a child for ten loaves. He trained at Woolgrove's Bakery in Heslington Rd and also did some work as a chef at Terry's in St. Helen's Square. This family business has now been handed over to his sons and daughter, who with his wife, have worked with him for many years.

He is well-known for his charitable work around York, making many cakes and breads for the community, such as the Evening Press Toy Fund, Children in Need and Press Guardian Angel Appeal. He makes giant bread wheatsheaves for harvest festival celebrations at St Chad's, festive bread Christmas trees for display, and also baked a commemorative chocolate sponge cake from an original Terry's recipe when Van Wilson's *The Story of Terry's* was launched, in 2009.

In May 2000 he hit the headlines when he tried to stop an armed man robbing the Post Office in Albemarle Rd. In 2005 he campaigned for a replacement post box in the wall of his shop, after the Post Office closed. In 2016 he rushed to help a pensioner who had collapsed in the street and performed CPR.

'Along to Queen Victoria St, we had Wright's butchers – ah, those pork pies and meat and tomato patties! I can smell and taste them now.' *(Derrick Gray).*

'During the war we used to queue at Wright's Butchers and you got to know by people saying, oh they got so so in… and she used to, wouldn't open door, and you could have got there and it had all gone, you know there might be some corned beef or different things that's off ration, liver was off ration, things like that.' *(Joan Jackman).*

'Wright's pork butchers, my mum used to buy their pork pies at Christmas and box them up and send them off to relatives. Of course in the war things were scarce, and they used to have the vans come and people used to queue at Wright's for the van coming to see what they had on.'*(David Meek).*

No. 135 Albemarle Rd (previously no. 63)
On the opposite corner of Queen Victoria St in 1901 this was the unusually named Haworth Haworth, grocer and shopkeeper, with a Post Office too, later William Northall in 1911. By 1922 it was

Junction of Albemarle Rd and Queen Victoria St around 1910, before the trams. On the left is the bootmaker Farmery and on the right the grocer/confectioner, possibly Haworth. Note the tall cast iron vent pipe. (Mike Pollard)

Herbert grocers and Post Office on Albemarle Rd around the 1920s. (Hugh Murray)

George Wilfred Herbert, who lasted until at least the war. In 1949 it was John Petch grocer, then Eric Crabtree from 1957 until 1973, then Jackson's. It was later Patrick's, Avey's/Spar, Lewis, Schofield's, Heap's, and The Post Box/PO. It finally closed in 2004, around the same time as the closure of the Post Office in Bishopthorpe Rd.

No. 137 Albemarle Rd (previously no. 65)
Currently Knavesmire Butchers

This was a chemists, 100 years ago, Charles Edward Scott in 1913, and then Tyreman Sturdy (1924–1930). It was Richardson's (1931–1949), then Prosser's (1951–1967). Later it was briefly Albemarle Rd Launderama, then Hallas Butchers in the 1980s, Mousley Butchers in the 1990s, and then Smail's. Mr A Swales now trades here as Knavesmire Butchers.

'Prosser's the chemist, he made his own cough mixture, but after so long they stopped him making it, because I think there was opium or something in it!' *(David Meek).*

No. 139 Albemarle Rd (previously no. 65)
Currently Brown's Bookmakers and the Corner Barbershop

For a brief period in the 1930s, W J Chippendale was trading as a newsagent on the corner here, after moving from across the road at no. 74. In 1953 it became a dry cleaners, first King's of York (1953–1961) then Clarke's of Retford (1963–1974). There followed a long line of bookies: Jones' Bookies, Bardy's Bookies, Smith's Bookies, Martin's Bookies, Wilson's Bookies, Joe Harris Racing, Harris & York Racing. In the 1990s this shop and no. 74 Westwood Terrace were then knocked into one to become South Bank Racing, subsequently Knavesmire Racing. It is now Brown's Bookmakers, but the corner shop is now The Corner Barbershop.

No. 153 Albemarle Rd, previously no. 79
Albert Helliwell was trading here from his back yard as a cycle repairer in the 1950s, closing in 1963.

No. 160 Albemarle Rd
The 1939 Register shows a dealer in sweets and tobacco, Mary A. Orman here.

York Racecourse at the Knavesmire

Horse racing in York dates back to Roman times, but racing at the Knavesmire started in 1731, when the racecourse transferred from Clifton Ings because of flooding there. On a darker side, legendary highwayman Dick Turpin was hanged on the Knavesmire on April 19, 1739, and a memorial is still there by the Tadcaster Rd. York architect John Carr designed and built the first grandstand in 1754, and the York Racecourse Committee was formed in 1842, introducing the Gimcrack Stakes in 1846. In 1851 a crowd estimated at 150,000 saw The Flying Dutchman, winner of the Derby and St Leger in 1849, beat Voltigeur, who took both races the following year, in the so-called Great Match. The modern era attendance record is 42,586 on a July Saturday in 2010.

In 1915 during World War I, the racecourse accommodated 1,500 soldiers of the 5th Reserve Cavalry regiment, sleeping in the Grandstand. New stands had been built in 1890, and further improvements were made in 1965, 1989, 1996 and 2003.

In 1982 York Racecourse hosted a visit from Pope John Paul II, who said open-air mass for more than 200,000 pilgrims.

The Racecourse with 180 stables has played host to Royal Ascot at York in 2005 and the Ladbroke's St Leger in 2006. It has won the award of Best Racecourse of the Year from the Racegoers Club nine times. The Group 1 Juddmonte International ranks number one of all thoroughbred horse races in Britain.

The Knavesmire pub

The profile of public houses in our area was shaped by a figure from a hundred years ago. Canon Argles of St Clement's arrived in the parish in 1871, an outspoken critic of alcohol and public houses, viewing drink as a social evil. Despite the large number of houses being built in the Bishopthorpe Rd area of York, he was able to use his influence to prevent public houses opening in South Bank until his death in 1920. But it was not until 1932 that the Knavesmire pub opened, after a licence had been granted to the J.J. Hunt Brewery of York, transferred from the Haymarket Tavern in Haymarket. This York brewery owned the pub until 1956.

John J. Hunt Ltd was founded by Joseph Hunt in 1834, with the Ebor Brewery in Aldwark in York, although malting appears to be its most successful element. A pub next door, the Ebor Vaults, was open from around 1841 until it closed in 1968. However the new leader, John Joseph Hunt, gradually built up the business, and from 1890 began to acquire public houses at a steady rate. Following the death of John J. Hunt in 1927, the company concentrated on building new public houses to serve York's expanding suburbs. In 1953 Cameron's Brewery acquired a controlling interest in John J. Hunt, which also owned the Scarborough & Whitby Breweries. The company ceased brewing in 1956 and the brewery was demolished in 1972. The Knavesmire is currently a Greene King pub.

In 1933 this pub was advertised as the Knavesmire Hotel, at South Bank Tram Terminus: '10 bedrooms, hot and cold water, private suites. Annual dinners and reunions a speciality. Parties of 100 can be catered for. Ideal rooms for wedding receptions, parties and 21st birthday parties. Lunches, teas and dinners are provided. A suggestion – You can entertain your friends without worry of Accommodation, Crockery and Cutlery or Staff.'

Since then there have been a number of licensed victuallers listed here: William Leetham Jervis, J Royce, the Hornbys, and Martha Bennett. Later Harry Natt then Peter Innes Harding, who died in mysterious circumstances at the pub after a burglary in August 1979.

It was still known as a hotel in 1975. The current licensees are Stuart and Lyndsay and they still have a Knavesmire function suite for events, with two large interconnecting rooms with private bar. They serve breakfasts on weekends and race days, and offer a free meeting room for local community groups.

Balmoral Terrace

Building started on Balmoral Terrace around 1902/3, albeit in limited blocks, which were mainly on the north side. Private street works for tarmacking and drainage for the new houses was carried out in 1903. The street was completed around 1909, and benefited from being on the new tram route from town a few years later.

Balmoral Terrace around 1910. (Keith Watson)

No. 1 Balmoral Terrace

The end house on the north east corner of the terrace with Bishopthorpe Rd was a well-known confectioner for a long time. From around 1928 until 1974 it was George Tanfield, in his later years also a grocer. After he finished it became Robinson's Takeaway, and then Fancy That! Costume Hire, until it closed in 1994.

> 'On Balmoral Terrace just before you get to Bishopthorpe Road, there was Tanfield's. Now he was a very high-class grocer, and I can always remember going there. They used to slice the bacon and all that business.' *(David Meek).*

No. 2 Balmoral Terrace

On the opposite corner, in the building now merged with the South Bank Medical Centre at the front, there was a hairdresser in the 1930s. In 1939 this was Allen's, advertising as a 'permanent wave specialist, from 10/6 to 21/-. We shall be pleased to meet you at the above address.' Later it became Gillott's, then Frank Castleden, then

Balmoral Terrace ca 1913, with tramlines installed. (Geoff Shearsmith)

Lucy Bull for a long time from 1953 to 1975. When she finished it was Warren's men's hairdresser, which finally closed in 1989.

No 9 Balmoral Terrace
Robert Bowman was listed here as a master butcher (shopkeeper) in 1939. His father had been a butcher in Goodramgate in 1911, and following the death of his father Robert applied to be a Freeman of the City in 1926, with the Goodramgate address. It may be that he lived in Balmoral Terrace in 1939, rather than trading from that address.

No. 12 Balmoral Terrace
This housed a doctor's surgery in the 1980s, with Dr. Brian Ormston. In 1989 it closed and his surgery moved around the corner into what is now the South Bank Medical Centre at 175 Bishopthorpe Rd.

No. 16 Balmoral Terrace
This was another hairdresser: Gillott's (1949–1953), then Rene Phillips (1955–1965). Montague Spray ran the barbers on the ground floor at this time before Rene's husband Joseph took over the barbers. Later it

was Pamela, ladies' hairdresser (1967–1975), His & Hers for Hair in the 1980s and His & Hers by Rozita in the 1990s. It closed in 2001.

No. 60 Balmoral Terrace

No 60 was on the corner of Trafalgar Street, a greengrocer for 80 years. Initially it was Arthur Jonas from 1905 until 1951, with Eleanor Jonas from 1949–1951. From 1953 to 1974 it was Miss E. Nicholson, and Fowler's fruiterers from 1974 until 1991 when it finally closed.

'I believe [Jonas] also kept a hen run where Count de Burgh Terrace is now.' *(Derrick Gray)*.

No. 61 Balmoral Terrace

There was another long-standing trade here, a draper's shop. In the 1911 census it was Eleanor Bell draper, and then in 1913 Reginald Stuart Vaughan, tailor. He was recorded as a draper until 1939, when intriguingly he was listed on the register as temporarily unemployed from a job as branch manager of an oil, paint and colour store, and his wife Clara Vaughan was recorded as 'drapery trade shopkeeper'. She was known locally as a high class ladies' outfitter, and following her death in 1962, the business seems to have stayed in the family as Vaughan Bennett until 1973 (they also had a shop at Regent Buildings in Acomb), then Pike's. It was Bridges & Fowler retail draper until 1980. At last with a change of trade it then became Rooke's Glass shop, then Janico's Bathroom Accessories, and then Pelman Distributors. It is currently connected to Janico across the road, as it is the registered office of the AMCO Management Company. AMCO and Janico have been providing electrical, heating, and plumbing wholesale services for over 40 years, starting as a small family business in this area of York in 1972.

No. 62/64 Balmoral Terrace
Currently Janico Electrical Supplies

York Equitable Industrial Society Ltd opened a shop here in Balmoral Terrace in 1902, built out of wood and corrugated iron on brick foundations, using fittings from other branches. There is still a plaque high on the front which proudly announces that 'this branch was opened by R D Hallam (Director) 19th March 1902'. The directors were authorised in 1900 to 'erect grocer's and butcher's shops and

York Equitable Industrial Society Ltd, grocery and butchering in Balmoral Terrace ca 1909. Now Janico. Note Trafalgar St undeveloped on the west side behind the shop. (Hugh Murray)

cottages on the plot of land agreed to be purchased at Balmoral Terrace on the South Bank Estate.' The Society had been offered the option of purchasing this plot when the estate was first being laid out and it was thought desirable to be the first in the field. A notice board had therefore been put up, warning all and sundry that 'it was the intention of the Society to build shops on the site; consequently, in this case at any rate, our competitors could have no grievance as to want of knowledge of the Society's designs for the new district, when the development warranted it'. The shop was quickly replaced by a more solid construction, and the surplus land sold for the building of the new adult school.

One of the founder members of the Society in York in 1858 was Robert Rathmell, who lived locally in Dale St. The Society had been slow to take off at first, with its prices regarded as uncompetitive for York workers with varying incomes. But once it became more successful, it antagonised local shopkeepers. Belonging to the 'Co-op' however became regarded as a statement of respectability, and they held a gala for members in 1907 on the Knavesmire, attracting around 30,000–40,000 people. The Society changed its name to the York Co-operative

Society from the 1940s, eventually merging in 1984 with the Harrogate Co-operative Society to become the North Yorkshire Co-operative Society.

The shop was still operating as a grocery and butchery in the 1980s, closing around 1985. No. 62 Balmoral Terrace was bought by Janico around 1996, when many of the Co-op buildings were being sold off (at some point nos. 62 and 64 had been amalgamated). Janico provides electrical, heating, and plumbing wholesale services. There are current plans however for Janico to relocate and there is an application for a change from retail use to an apartment block.

'Yes, the Co-op used to deliver milk and groceries with horses...our horse that came to my mum's, was called Robin, and one of the milkmen that we had was Arthur Bottom. He was a famous footballer and, they [York City] in 1955 got into the semi-finals with Newcastle, and they lost but afterwards the referee admitted that he'd been got at. And Arthur Bottom, he brought my mum's milk the morning of the big match. And everyone was saying "All the best Arthur", and he was saying, "We'll do our best". And he used to say that the horse knew the round better than he did. They used to walk round and the horse would just stop. They used to back the horses in at the Co-op and the horses could back them in theirselves. I don't know how they did it because it's a dreadful job backing in a horse and cart.' *(David Meek).*

No. 75 Balmoral Terrace
Currently closed

Another corner shop, at the junction with Count de Burgh Terrace, was an early grocer, Joseph Easey from 1909. William Robinson took over in 1922 and lasted until 1939, when Harold Kirby took his place. By 1949 it was A E Thorns, who lasted until the mid-1980s, later Cox & Taylor off-licence, then Dave's, Hall's, J & M, and then Cox's Corner Shop. Until recently it was known as South Bank Stores, but has been closed for a while. The new owner has plans to open the shop again next year.

Brunswick Street

Building started on what is now Brunswick St in 1900, and William Chapman de Burgh was involved with at least some of the houses. Nos. 2–24 were built in what was then known as Brunswick Rd, changing to St a little later. Two smaller streets, Hubert St and Ruby St, were created on the north side. Private street works were carried out in 1903 for tarmacking and drainage for the new houses. There remained a gap in the houses for many years, as an area of Brunswick St on the north side had been sold by De Burgh to John J Hunt in 1898, possibly with a view to a new pub there. Much later, in 1934, this site was sold by the executors of J.J. Hunt's will to John Norman Dunn, architect, and houses were built (now nos. 51–59).

The alleyway described locally as 'The Sleepers' was widened from its original width, and this may have been when old railway sleepers were replaced by stone paviours. The 1898 conveyance notes "The 10 feet road on western boundary to be extended to 20 feet width – made and completed to the satisfaction of York Corporation".

Yvonne Evans remembers standing on the corner of Brunswick St on race days collecting car number plates.

No. 1A/2A Brunswick St

This address, on the corner of Count de Burgh Terrace, appears to have been a private house until the 1960s, when it was South Bank Launderette. It later became Shuttleworth Motor Bike Spares, then Audio Clinic, Riley Electronics, Direct Workwear Store, and Collinson's. It finally closed in 2002.

No. 5 Brunswick St

No 5 was an end terrace, on the angle as the road turns. Another long-standing trader, John Blakeborough, was listed as a hairdresser in 1905, and lasted over fifty years as a gents' hairdresser, until closing in 1961. He appears to have been a well-known character.

'Blakeborough's barber's shop – haircut and shave six old pence. When he had no customers he sat at the front door playing the mandolin.' (Derrick Gray).

'He used to cut hair in his front room. If he wasn't too busy, he used to sit on the step and play a banjo. I think for a boy it was about eight pence for a haircut, my dad used to call it an "Eight penn'orth all off"! His daughter ended up working for the dogs' home. She used to bring the dogs home to walk them.' *(David Meek)*.

Nos.16/18 Brunswick St
In 1906 a butcher's shop and dwelling house was offered for sale here.

No. 49 Brunswick St
This was another old shop, with Ada Eccles running it in 1911, as her husband Charles was paralysed at 42. By the 1920s it was a general dealer Riby Wilson, who was trading until around the outbreak of war. His family stayed in the house, possibly not keeping it as a shop.

No. 62 Brunswick St
This was one of the local dairymen, Milky Dave, from around 1970. He originally worked for the Co-operative Dairy until it finished, then bought the milk round from them.

No. 81 Brunswick St
A grocer's shop over a long period, with Walter Paul selling dairy produce in the 1930s, then Malloy's from around 1939 until 1950, followed by Mrs Nickson in the 1950s and Mrs Thompson in the 1960s and 1970s. It closed in 1977.

No. 85 Brunswick St
This is a comparatively new building, extending from the backyard of 129 Albemarle Road. From around 1984 it has housed a series of businesses: Business Travel, Securicor, Vodaphone, a photography office, and then Amy's Canine Centre around 2004. In recent years it became The Box Barbershop, which closed in 2019, to be absorbed into an extension for D & K Stores. The barber has now moved to 139 Albemarle Rd.

No. 118 Brunswick St
No 118 was a butcher from 1901, Fred Thompson, certainly until 1913, and then became a long-standing boot- and shoe-repairer, William Hodgson in the 1920s, R Farmery in the 1930s and then Arthur Featherstone from around 1951 to 1968. Subsequently it was

Thompson's fruit and veg in the 1970s, then a model makers shop, then Gillian York dress fitters for around 20 years, closing in the 1990s.

Mrs Gillian Shuttleworth, who grew up in Brunswick St, bought the house and shop in 1976 from Newitt's, who also had a large sports shop in Goodramgate. Her previous business had been in rented premises in Count de Burgh Terrace, where she had her first soft toymaking/dress alteration shop (now rebuilt as Percy Mews). In Brunswick St she had a self-contained shop and toilet, and when she moved in she had a door knocked through to the kitchen and lived above and behind the shop. She ran a very successful dress alteration business, with people coming from miles around. She also sold wool and made quality teddy bears in the colours of many northern football clubs, including Manchester United, which were bought by clubs for sale in their shops. She even adapted the teddy into an owl for Sheffield Wednesday. Eventually she had the premises converted back into a whole house in the mid-1990s when she retired.

No. 120 Brunswick St
This is a slightly confusing address, as it is next to the end door on Brunswick St, now listed as 131 Albemarle Rd. In 1901 no.120 was a house and shop, the latter belonging to Susan Rose, a fancy draper from 1901 to 1905, and then draper Elizabeth Gibson. In the 1920s, no.120 disappears from the listings, but the next house and shop, listed as Albemarle House, was Thomas Farmery, bootmaker/shopkeeper in 1901, whose door may have been on Albermarle Rd. His shop sign appears on old photographs around this time (see no. 131 Albemarle Rd).

Campleshon Road
Campleshon Lane appears to have been named after Leonard Campleshon, Clerk of Ripley, as in 1642 the Dean and Chapter of York granted him a lease of Nun Fields and Nun Ings. A skull and a coin of Claudius Gothicus have been found in this area.

The road appears on photographs as a narrow track or lane for many years, eventually bolstered by the construction of Knavesmire School in 1916 and St Chad's Church in 1925/6. Work started on the widening and re-alignment of Campleshon Lane, moving to the south, to

Campleshon Lane at the Bishopthorpe Rd junction, before it was realigned and enlarged.
(Hugh Murray)

become Campleshon Rd by 1926. Lorne St was built in 1936, between the school and the church. In 1984 plans were passed for the Viking Housing Society to build three housing blocks for the elderly at the rear of St. Chad's Church.

'Amongst my earliest memories, whilst walking out with my mother, was a single track railway running down Campleshon Rd and up to Terry's. Tip-over trucks ran along this, carrying soil from Terry's. I think the one-storey factory was being built at the time. I must confess I have no idea where this rail track ended or even where the rail went.' *(Derrick Gray).*
'I was told it was used to carry spoil dug out when creating the foundations for the multi-storey factory. The rails were laid as far as the Knavesmire where the spoil was tipped.' *(Keith Watson).*

No. 4 Campleshon Road

At the eastern end of Campleshon Rd there was a dairy and grocer's for many years, first Lacey's in the 1930s and then Dyson's in the 1950s, followed by Moore's, then Norman's in the 1960s and Turner's in the 1970s. By 1990 it was South Bank Video, then the Institute of Physics and Engineering in Medicine in the late 1990s, which subsequently moved to Tadcaster Road. Later it became known as Knavesmire House, with a chartered surveyors, Barton Laverick, Phillips, who are now at Front St, in Acomb. It appears to have changed hands last in 2004.

The Church of St Chad on the Knavesmire

To meet the spiritual and pastoral needs of a rapidly growing
population in South Bank, the South Bank Mission Chapel had been
built in South Bank Ave (see no.88a) in 1900, as an outreach centre
for St. Clement's Church in Scarcroft Rd. This was a multi-purpose
building functioning primarily as a place of worship.

In 1920 the Parochial Church Council of St Clement's passed a
resolution that a new church be built in South Bank as a memorial
to Canon Argles, who had served for over 40 years as vicar of St
Clement's, and who had died in that year. Colonel Wood of Old
Nunthorpe donated a portion of land near Campleshon Lane in 1920,
and the York Race Committee added to it in 1923. Additional land
was conveyed in 1926. The new 'Argles Memorial Church' would be
dedicated to St Chad.

Money was raised by local subscriptions and also many fund-raising
initiatives, including a 'Buy A Brick' campaign, Thank-offering Days
and several bazaars. A three-day 'Model Market' was held in the
Assembly Rooms in 1922 and opened by the Countess of Harewood,
raising over £1500.

St Chad's Church under construction.

Plans were drawn up by the celebrated architect Walter Brierley in 1924, and building started on the new church, officially named the Church of St. Chad on the Knavesmire. The widow of Canon Argles laid the foundation stone in May 1925 and the church was completed in 1926 at a cost of £10,300.

Archbishop Lang consecrated the church on 9 October 1926. The church is built in brick throughout and comprises a nave, originally intended as a chancel, of three bays with a Lady Chapel at the east end. The present structure represents only half the original plan, of which many features were left uncompleted, including the tower, due to a lack of funding. In 1928 the parish of St. Chad was created from portions of both the parishes of St Mary Bishophill Senior and Holy Trinity Micklegate, and the Reverend George Boddy was instituted as the first vicar in the same year.

St Chad's Greys Scout Troop was set up in 1927 and in 1947 Fred Weatherley and Bryan Jowsey formed St Chad's Greys Scout Band. In 2001 the Scouts hut was completely destroyed by fire and was replaced by a temporary structure still used by the troop today.

St Chad's Church, opened 1926.

In 1930 St Chad's Church purchased the building on Count de Burgh Terrace built in 1903 as South Bank Adult School. Today it is home to St Clement's Working Men's Club. It was used for many years as a church hall, but was finally sold in 1967 to fund the completion of the west end of St Chad's church, 41 years after the church was first consecrated. In 1970 a new church hall was built alongside the west end. The Church is a Grade II listed building due to its innovative structural form.

Knavesmire Primary School

South Bank Temporary School had opened in 1906 at the St. Clement's Mission Room in South Bank Ave, and by 1911 South Bank Temporary Infants School opened in the premises of the Adult School in Balmoral Terrace. By 1914 there were 159 children enrolled in the two temporary schools, and a new, purpose-built school was much needed in the area, to serve its growing population, including children in Cherry St and Scarcroft Schools waiting to transfer.

Designed by the Bolton architect J.T. Proffitt, the new Knavesmire Council School opened in Campleshon Rd in 1916, with a capacity of 800. Extensions, including a new wing, were added in 1931 to create 160 extra places. In 1945 the school was split into a primary school for infants and secondary modern school for girls.

The school previously had its own canteen in a single storey building across the other side of the end of Trafalgar St, but this was demolished to make way for new housing in the 1990s.

By 1963 construction began on a new secondary modern school near to Bustardthorpe, and this opened for girls in 1964, and boys in 1965. Local educational reforms led to its closure in 1985, and the building became York College of Law in 1989, who relocated to Leeds in 2014. Since then it has housed the York Campus of OneSchool Global UK, an independent educational trust.

In 2014 the final phase of the Primary School extensions in South Bank was completed by William Birch & Co, including a canteen, new hall, and additional teaching spaces. In 2016 Knavesmire Primary School became part of South Bank Multi-Academy Trust.

Knavesmire Crescent, December 1953.

St Clement's AFC 1947 (Geoff Shearsmith).
Back row: J.E. Wright (President), T. Moyser, J. Trimble, G.O. Pickup, W. Smith (Hon Sec),
G.E. Hodgson (Captain), C.E. Berry, S. Richardson (Trainer)
Front row: W.B. Shaw, A. Lyall, G.S. Winters, J.R. Shaw, D. Kirk.

View of Albemarle Rd from the Knavesmire. (Geoff Shearsmith)

Count de Burgh

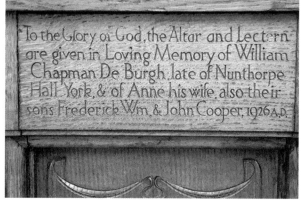

Memorial carving to William Chapman de Burgh on the altar of St Chad's Church. (Susan Major)

Count de Burgh Terrace

This terrace was named after a famous local businessman, 'Count' William Chapman de Burgh. Born in 1840 locally in Bishophill, he became a 'Land Agent' in the 1880s. His name was originally William Chapman, but rather mysteriously in 1890 he changed it officially by deed poll to William Chapman de Burgh, later adding the prefix Count. His father George was described at different times as an architect, joiner and cabinet maker, and surveyor, and it appears that William became considerably wealthy during his life from quite humble circumstances, by speculating in land and property in our area. William died in 1901, and is buried in York Cemetery, but 'Messrs De Burgh' were still developing locally in 1913. One of his sons, Harold, went on to be Sheriff and then Lord Mayor of York in the 1940s. Another son, Arthur, seems to have had less luck, becoming bankrupt in 1902. There is a memorial carving to the De Burgh family on the altar at St Chad's.

The first two houses in Count de Burgh Terrace appear around 1902–1909, and private street works for tarmacking and drainage for new houses were carried out in 1919. In 1934 Relton Bros builders started building work on the lower end houses, on land purchased from the De Burgh estate.

No .2 Count de Burgh Terrace

No. 2 housed a confectioner and cake maker, Thomas Craven Hutchinson, for many years. He was first listed in 1911, probably shortly after this end of the street was built. He was still at this address until his death in 1941.

No. 3 Count de Burgh Terrace

This address housed a grocer, Joseph Easey, in 1911, but by 1913 the shop had been renumbered to become 75 Balmoral Terrace. (See Balmoral Terrace).

No. 13 Count de Burgh Terrace

In the 1950s this was South Bank Fisheries, at times known as The Hut and The Dukeries. It was apparently built on behalf of the de Burgh family for a Mrs. Smith as a fish shop, passing on later to Bernard Powell. In the 1970s it became Grainger's Hardware, later Scott's Hardware and DIY. Finally it was Bespoke Upholstery Services in the

1990s, closing in 2005. There appears to have been briefly a further fish and chip shop at no. 17 Count de Burgh Terrace in the late 1930s, Bernard Harrison Powell. Did he move along to no. 13?

'Powell's fish and chip shop, Mr and Mrs Powell…and in the war they couldn't get fish and all sorts, but if they could get some the word would go round South Bank "Have you heard, Powell's are opening tonight.' *(David Meek)*.

This site was demolished along with houses on the corner of Brunswick St, and a terrace of new houses, Percy Mews, built in 2011.

St Clement's Working Men's Club today. (Susan Major)

St Clement's Working Men's Club

St Clement's Working Men's Club was founded and opened in 1900 using two cottages at 1 and 3 Queen Victoria Street, on the northern corner of Queen Victoria Street and Count De Burgh Terrace, in properties owned by William Chapman De Burgh. It was originally designed as a reading and debating room. It was affiliated to the Club & Institute Union in 1908.

The building now known as St. Clement's Club, on the corner of Balmoral Terrace and Count de Burgh Terrace, was built in 1903 as

South Bank Adult School, by the Trustees of the Adult School and Social Union, 'so that democracy might enjoy wisely in a spiritual atmosphere its leisure moments'. Moves for adult education in York were led by the Society of Friends (Quakers) with members of the Rowntree family, and a large number were created in York around the turn of the 20th century. They were supported by York Educational Settlement and deliberately presented as an alternative for the working classes to the public house, at the same time encouraging people into organised religion.

It was used by many different organisations, for example in 1906 it hosted an art exhibition, with many paintings lent by residents, and three samplers worked by the Brontë sisters. That year a new hall extension was built and opened, and by 1910 meetings of the York Society of Friends started in the Adult School, known as the South Bank Meeting. These lasted until 1918.

From 1911 it functioned as a children's school, before Knavesmire School was built in 1916, and Workers Educational Association evening classes were also held here. The South Bank Mission of St. Clement's parish used it as a Church Hall that year too. In 1926 it was secured as the new headquarters of the York Toc H, an international movement originally set up to support servicemen, which had moved from St William's College. It was also used as a gymnasium by the South Bank and LNER Football teams. The building was later bought by St Chad's Church and after refurbishment used as their hall from 1931.

'In World War II in 1940, after Dunkirk, the hall was taken over by the military, for soldiers returning from France. It was used mainly as a Forces canteen, with people cooking outside on open fires. There was also a corrugated construction used by St. Clement's Football Club for changing, known as The Tabernacle, because of its many-sided shaped pointed roof.

'The main building was also a Forces recreational centre. The Hall cellar and boiler room was K3, the local Air Raid Warden's post. This post was eventually moved to the land at the junction of Balmoral Terrace and Bishopthorpe Rd, tacked on to an air raid shelter. After the Forces moved out, it was used as a civic restaurant, very useful for workers, particularly for working mums. It helped to spread the rations a bit. Spam was usually the prominent meat, accompanied by what was known as bread in battledress – sausages! I was put off sausages for many years after those wartime monstrosities.' (*Derrick Gray*)

In 1966 the building was sold to St. Clement's Club for £9,500, with the proceeds used towards completion of the unbuilt church tower at St Chad's. It appears that the club was in a tied contract at its original premises under Cameron's Brewery (successors to J.J. Hunt Brewery), and only able to move over here once the contract had expired. An application was submitted for alterations to turn the Hall into a Club, which opened in 1972.

In 1975 the Club submitted an application for alterations and extensions, and in 1976 opened a new lounge bar. There was further work carried out in 1984 and in 1991.

By January 2012 however the Club was in severe financial difficulties, on the brink of closure with large debts. New Club Secretary Raymond Fligg came in and rescued it, putting it on a sound financial footing, supported by Treasurer Andrew Franks. The former steward's house was sold to meet debts. St Clement's received a national award in 2013 from the CIU, as the best turned-round club in Great Britain, a tremendous achievement.

It has a lounge, a bar and a snooker room upstairs, and currently has around 450 members. Activities include quizzes, dominoes, snooker, pool, bingo, raffles and live music.

Curzon Terrace

The first houses were built here in 1900, with houses on the east side of the terrace. The De Burgh family applied for planning permission for six cottages in the street in 1904. Nos 1–24 were built in 1900, then up to 52 by 1902, then up to 79 by 1913.

The street had a surprising number of shops around the 1930s.

No.6 Curzon Terrace

Alice Bootland was a shop keeper at the first terrace house, from 1901 until 1909. She then seems to have moved across the road to 34 Knavesmire Crescent.

No.9 Curzon Terrace

This trader first appears in the listings in 1935, Thomas Blake Griffin, a dairyman, born in 1905. Later there were two brothers at Griffin's Dairy, Tom and Jim, sons of Thomas Griffin. They are remembered as delivering the milk in a horse and trap. They kept their horses in a stables building accessed by the lane between 49–51 Brunswick Street which later became a studio flat and the horses were also kept in a field which in the 1980s had houses built on it, forming the current St. James' Mount off Albermarle Road. The business closed in 1978.

No.14 Curzon Terrace

Norman Harlow Stirling Latham was a confectioner in the 1920s, but then the family moved to 34 Knavesmire Crescent in 1925. They seem to have swapped houses with Austin and Alice Bootland, bakers, around 1913 at 34 Knavesmire Crescent, as the Bootland family were listed here at Curzon Terrace from 1925 until 1965.

No. 22 Curzon Terrace

In the 1930s Harry Lacy was recorded as living here and also briefly as a confectioner next door at no.24. Paul Burke delivered milk from the house from 1991, closing in 2005.

No.42 Curzon Terrace

William Bradley was a grocer and confectioner from 1922 until the late 1930s.

No.79 Curzon Terrace

This was a shop in 1913, when William Holmes traded as a grocer until 1925. By 1939 Lillie Dawson was recorded as the grocer. In 1944 this address was offered for sale as a shop and dwelling house, with the shop in place of a front sitting room, let to Miss Dawson at a net annual rent of £20.8s.8d.

The current owner, Chris Holmes (no relation) found markings on the wall when he was renovating the property, indicating the house has been a shop for forty years from 1913, shortly after it was built, until 1953.

Kensington St
The first houses were built in 1900, after Chapman de Burgh had applied for planning permission for 75 cottages in the street in 1899. Private street works for tarmacking and drainage for the new houses were completed in 1903. In 1934 Relton Bros builders started building work on the lower end houses, on land purchased from the De Burgh estate.

No. 2a Kensington St
The house on the north east end, next to the back alleyway, was Pailey's, a general dealer and 'vegetable hawker' in 1939, lasting until 1963, when he closed. Locals remember his house shop selling groceries and sweets. However Mr. Pailey is best remembered for trailing up and down outside the Empire Theatre (now the Grand Opera House), selling his wares from a large basket: 'Don't forget your Wrigley's, toffees, peanuts and oranges' was the cry.

No. 4 Kensington St
Thomas Rushton had a shop here in 1909.

No. 32 Kensington St
There was a long-standing tailor here, Joseph Hudson, recorded from 1937. It appears his business, Hudson's Tailoring, closed in 1960, but he remained at the house at least until 1975.

No. 37 Kensington St
Harry Lacey had a shop here in 1902.

Knavesmire Crescent
A few houses at the north end of Knavesmire Crescent were built by 1900, but most were built several years later, for example Messrs De Burgh submitted an application for four houses in 1910. There were private street works for tarmacking and drainage for the new houses in 1916. In 1908 a new gate was erected to the Knavesmire.

No.34 Knavesmire Crescent
This is the house on the corner of Curzon Terrace, where the Bootlands and the Lathams appear to have swapped with 14 Curzon Terrace, just over the road.

Bootland Bakers (Alice) were here in the 1911 census, and then in 1913 and up to 1924. Then it became Latham's. G A Latham was a confectioner from 1928, then Norman Harlow Stirling Latham from 1939–65. Intriguingly Norman was listed as a railway carriage repair carpenter in the 1939 Register, and therefore it may have been his wife who ran the shop. From 1968 it was McMahon's sweet shop, which lasted until 1993.

'Latham's shops for sweets, you know, and we used to go to this shop mostly, next door. They sold sweets, all that…she used to have trays, one with halfpenny sweets in and one with penny and I've been in and the children had a penny, they'd spend ages. She used to say 'will you hurry up', she was waiting for them to choose halfpenny sweets.' *(Joan Jackman).*

Montague St
The first houses in Montague St were built in 1900 on the north east corner of the street. There was a planning application in from Messrs De Burgh in 1911/13 for 12 cottages and a house in the street. Work on the lower end houses started in 1934, by Relton Bros builders, on land bought from the De Burgh estate.

No. 1a Montague St
This shop was on the north west end of the terrace, on the corner of the back alleyway leading to Kensington St. It was firstly a jeweller and grocer in 1932, recorded as Cyril Alfred Latham and still there in 1939, when he seems to have reverted to his birth name, Cyril Alfred Foster. He later moved to 145 Bishopthorpe Rd by 1949, until at least 1975.

The shop became a range of grocers, Cadamy's until 1951, briefly Hillyard's and also Clinton's in the 1950s, Warrington's (1955–59), Watson's (1961), W & E Ellis (1963–65), then Davis's from 1967, until it closed in 1974.

Queen Victoria St
Construction began around 1900 and completed by around 1903, with private street works for tarmacking and drainage for the new houses. Press reports highlighted the demand for a smaller class of houses, with tenants wanting to enter even before the plaster was dry on new builds. Queen Victoria St became a hive of trading activity, with many shops on the corners and along the terraced rows of house fronts.

You can still see the shadows in the bricks as you walk along, with surprisingly as many as twenty shops along here in various decades.

> 'You could buy a kite-shaped bag with 'Kayli' in it. It was a flavoured powder and when you dipped your finger in it, it fizzed in your mouth when licked. Sometimes these bags had a stick of liquorice in them, but you could also get these with a clay pipe. Your clay pipe was then used to blow soap bubbles, using of course soap flakes to make the suds.' (Derrick Gray).

On 30 July 1913, the South Bank tram route opened, with three electric trams running from the Station along Bishopthorpe Rd and up Balmoral Terrace and Queen Victoria St, to turn at Albemarle Rd. Powered from overhead cables, each blue and cream vehicle took up to 48 passengers on two floors – the top open to the elements. Work was later carried out in the street in 1918, widening and resurfacing, to an average width of 28ft.

A wartime shortage of male staff led to the trams' brakes being fitted with gearing, making them easier for women to operate. The trams ran till 1935, when they were replaced by buses.

> 'I remember trams. When it was race day you used to be queuing on Queen Victoria St because they had two, they drove this way and then they went back and drove from that end and they used to let us play on them on race days because they waited for all races to finish.' (Joan Jackman).

No. 1 and 3 Queen Victoria St
On the north west corner of Queen Victoria St and Count De Burgh Terrace, St Clement's Working Men's Club was founded and opened in 1908 at 1 and 3 Queen Victoria St, in property originally owned by William Chapman de Burgh. It lasted there until 1969, when it moved over the road into larger premises on the south east corner with Count de Burgh Terrace. You can still see the pattern in the brickwork changing on this corner.

No. 2 Queen Victoria St
On the opposite corner with Count de Burgh Terrace was a long-standing newsagents from around 1913, Rowland Lemmon, later Frank Hersey in the 1920s. You can still see the shape of the large

staff and military service. The building suffered war damage, set on fire by three bombs hitting the roof and chimney stacks, and impassable chasms were left in the driveway.

Nunthorpe Court eventually became the home of Richard's son, Sir Algar De Clifford Charles Meysey-Thompson, who sold the house in 1920 to York Corporation, along with 11 acres of land, for £10,750, a relatively low amount at the time. Algar then moved to live in the lodge at the Nunthorpe Ave entrance, where he died aged 82 in 1967. Approximately 22 acres of land from the old estate were sold in 1935 to Harry and Louise Williamson from Heworth Green, and the Nunthorpe estate was developed, with many houses in Nunthorpe Grove and Nunthorpe Crescent selling for £475.

The Council opened Nunthorpe Court Secondary School for Boys in 1920, much needed because of a great demand for secondary education for boys at this time, with the overcrowding at Archbishop Holgate's School. At that time however less than 5% of boys in primary education in York went on to secondary education. When it opened the school had 49 boys, of whom 27 were fee-paying.

The school grew quickly. In 1927 a north-west wing was added as a hall/gymnasium, with another new hall and quadrangle in 1937. The Corporation also bought Mill Mount House for £8,000 for use as a girls' school. The two schools could each accommodate 200 pupils.

The start of the autumn term in 1939 was delayed because of the need to strengthen the cellars for air raid shelters. In the 1942 Baedeker air raid on York most of the windows at the front of the old building were smashed, and a member of staff was killed. The kitchen was damaged by the falling engine of a Halifax bomber which exploded in mid-air.

The 1944 Education Act led to a change from secondary school for boys to boys' grammar school, and in 1950 it was renamed Nunthorpe Grammar School. There were further additions: a new block of classrooms in 1959, a sixth form block in 1974 and a sports hall in 1984. In 1985, as York went comprehensive, Nunthorpe and Mill Mount schools merged to become Millthorpe School, with pupils from other York schools joining. The school is now part of the South Bank Academy Trust.

Kentmere House and 1 Telford Terrace
Now Kentmere Art Gallery and offices for MCA Funding for Churches

Kentmere House, on the corner of Scarcroft Hill and Telford Terrace, was the home of the Primitive Methodist Chapel Aid Association (PMCAA). This was set up in 1890 by Sir William Pickles Hartley of Hartley's Jam, to raise money for loan to debt-ridden chapels on the cheapest terms. At this time there was a boom in chapel-building and the Primitive Methodists had debts of over £1 million. York was chosen as its base because of railway links with Northern towns, where its directors, all businessmen, lived. It was based first at 63 Bishopthorpe Rd, but later moved to Telford Terrace in January 1900. The house had been built in 1898 and there is still an inscribed stone to that effect built into the front of the house.

Kentmere House today. (Susan Major)

Kentmere House accommodated its Secretary, with a separate wing for the housekeeper and nursery, with offices and boardroom next door, and a connecting door. There was a small strong room with two-foot thick walls, where they kept the chapel deeds while loans were outstanding. This was demolished in the late 1990s (once deeds had been computerised by the Land Registry) to provide additional office space. The entire property was later sold in 1983, PMCAA retaining a lease on the office area. The lease has been renewed and PMCAA, now operating as MCA Funding for Churches, is still at 1 Telford Terrace and now supports churches of all denominations.

For four years prior to 1991 the house was occupied by Madeleine Evans, a homeopath and since 1991 the house has become the Kentmere House Art Gallery, owned by Ann and David Petherick, chosen because of its large rooms with high ceilings and a spacious staircase – perfect for displaying original art. Ann's previous gallery was at Grape Lane.

Nunthorpe Hall

Nunthorpe Hall was demolished over 40 years ago, thus many will not know of it or perhaps confuse it with Nunthorpe Court, which still stands. It was designed and built in 1866/7 by local architect Herbert Fippard, for mining engineer Henry Johnson McCulloch. Plans called it 'South Bank House' or 'Captain McCulloch's Mansion'. The Hall was on an elevated position overlooking the little Knavesmire, reached from a long driveway off Bishopthorpe Rd.

McCulloch was a prominent York citizen with a reputation for commercial interests, following employment by the North Eastern Railway. He was involved with philanthropic movements, a founder of Elmfield College, and a guarantor of the York Exhibition of 1886. He was prominent in the Primitive Methodist Church and a Liberal councillor for Micklegate ward in the 1860s. However following unsuccessful speculation he had to sell the mansion soon after and left York in 1868. But his fortunes revived and he became consulting engineer to the Admiralty.

The sale particulars describe 'a handsome and commodious residence… overlooking Knavesmire, replete with every modern accessory of reception, domestic and culinary arrangement, together with Garden and Stable requirement'. Plans included provision for a game larder, a meat larder and a china closet at the rear of the ground floor behind the entrance hall. The gardens extended down to Albemarle Rd and bordered the entire length of Philadelphia Terrace.

Nunthorpe Hall. (Hugh Murray)

The carriage drive to Bishopthorpe Rd had a lodge and 'tasteful' entrance gates, opening into an avenue of chestnut, lime and sycamore trees, around 600 yards long. This road was originally described in maps as The Avenue, but when houses were built on it in the early 1900s it was renamed South Bank Avenue.

Nunthorpe Hall was sold at auction in 1870 to Mr J A Reim of Sunderland, for £6,200. Subsequently the Armitage family were there in the 1870s, and Isaac Wilson in 1879. But there is some surprising evidence from 1881 and 1885 that local property speculator William Chapman, the famous 'Count de Burgh' was living there in that period, and a memorial to him at St Chad's Church from 1926 refers to him as being 'late of Nunthorpe Hall'.

A family of wealthy industrialists, the Lycett-Green's, moved to York in 1888 to live at Nunthorpe Hall. Their fortunes had been made by Edward Green, who had bought the invention of a successful fuel economiser from a Leeds engineer in 1843, and used his business acumen to make a fortune from it, together with his son, Edward Lycett-Green, who became the 1st baronet. The latter became a good friend of King Edward, as their Norfolk estates were alongside each other. His son, Edward, the 2nd Bt and wife Ethel Lycett-Green were involved in the famous baccarat scandal at Tranby Croft, near Hull, in 1890, involving the Prince of Wales.

bricked-up window. Frank seems to have moved to 29 Queen Victoria St in the late 1920s, possibly on retirement.

Lemmon's advert in the Southlands Messenger in January 1914 ironically says '1914 is now with us. To make this year a year free from worry, and every day a joy day, order all your Newspapers and Periodicals from R. Lemmon's'.

By 1939 the newsagent was William Chippendale, who also sold stationery and tobacco, and had previously been in Albemarle Rd. His advert that year says 'We all make mistakes but I do endeavour to deliver newspapers, both morning and evening, promptly'.

The newsagent changed to Slater's after the war, bought by Fred Slater in 1947. He worked in the newsagent's until ill health forced him to give it up and his eldest daughter, Barbara and husband Ron continued to run it. The shop was heated with coal fires and staff communicated with customers through hatches. Fred's wife Mary owned the property until the late 1970s. However in 1977 Barbara died suddenly and Ron took it over in partnership with John Chambers, who was married to Barbara and Ron's daughter Gillian. In 1978 it became South Bank Newsagents. Ron eventually left the business in

St Clement's Pipe Club outing, ca 1920s. (Geoff Shearsmith)

1990 and John continued to run it as a newsagent's until 2003, when it was converted into a house where John and Gillian lived until 2017.

There was a large advertising hoarding on the wall facing Count De Burgh Terrace in the later years and you can still see the outline of where it was on the brickwork today.

No. 5 Queen Victoria St
Next to the original Working Men's Club, at no 5, John Cryer sold fish and chips and wet fish as early as 1911. In the 1930s it was fish dealer Anthony Alexander, known as Anthony's Fish and Chips. He closed in 1953. It must have been a small shop as there is nothing revealed in brickwork.

No. 6 Queen Victoria St
Henry Smith had a shop here in 1901.

No. 12 Queen Victoria St
The Chapman family were recorded here as early as 1923. Harry Chapman was a tailor in 1939 and then in 1953 for a few years it was listed as Chapman's Corsetière, one of two in the area, with Mrs Isobel Chapman. The business closed in 1959.

No. 17/19 Queen Victoria St
Elizabeth Matthew was a newsagent here in 1909, followed by Rowland Lemmon in 1911, before he moved to no. 2. Then followed a range of traders, first a confectioner's at no.19 with Ms Annie Richardson, and then general dealer Mrs Galtry in the 1920s, followed by Percy Danby then Horace Danby. After the war it was E E Dale, grocer, and then Mrs Brewis, expanding into no.17. By 1957 it was Smith's, and then in the 1970s Rooke's, closing in 1975. There are some brickwork changes.

'Smith's, that was a grocer's, and eventually he gave up and he went to be the butler at Castle Howard.' (*David Meek*).

No. 35 Queen Victoria St
This housed a butcher and slaughterer in 1939, Charles Moore. He was still recorded here after the war in 1949/50, but as a private resident.

The grocer on the corner of Butcher Terrace and Bishopthorpe Rd around 1990, with outside vending machines. (Karen Thompson)

Gillian soft toy manufacturer, at 118 Brunswick St. (Gillian Shuttleworth)

Fred's Bakery in Albemarle Rd.

Charles Symington, restoration bookbinder, in his workshop at 145 Bishopthorpe Rd.

Charles with his father Douglas, also a bookbinder.

RIVERSIDE LODGE HOTEL, 292 BISHOPTHORPE ROAD, YORK.

Riverside Lodge Hotel on Bishopthorpe Rd, now flats. (Keith Watson)

The Ashcroft Hotel at time of demolition, in 2001. (Keith Watson).

No. 37 Queen Victoria St

Here was a baker, confectioner and cake maker listed in 1939, Arnold Arundale, but it is not clear if this was a job rather than a shop.

No. 57 Queen Victoria St

The Carter family lived here from the 1920s, and in the 1930s Harold Carter was listed as a 'tripe dresser'. After the war it was Carter's grocers, and also remembered as Mrs. Carter's wet fish shop, a 'house shop', for many years, finally closing in 1955.

No. 62 Queen Victoria St

Maurice Overend was living here from around 1929, and recorded as a boot and shoe repairer from 1935, lasting for a lengthy period until he eventually closed in 1974. It was next to a back alleyway, and you can still see a large bricked-up shop window.

No. 63 Queen Victoria St

This house adjoined a back alleyway, and there are some changes to the brickwork. In 1937 F. Oglesby was briefly a fruiterer here. It was well-known as Mountain's Radio Repairs in the 1950s, then Radio Services Ltd, closing in 1959.

No. 65/67 Queen Victoria St

The other side of the alleyway there are brickwork changes, with another double house shop. No. 65 was a grocer's as long ago as 1901, with Elizabeth Hutchinson, still there in 1913. In the 1920s it was Walter Prest, general dealer. By 1938 Francois Auguste Gaget and his wife Alice were grocers trading from both addresses. After the war it was A J Mowforth until 1973, then Hudson's briefly, closing in 1975.

No. 90 Queen Victoria St

This was the receiving office for the Wenlock Laundry Ltd. in 1913. This company was based in Ambrose St, off Wenlock Terrace in York from around 1890. They seemed a successful business, constantly advertising for staff and expanding their Fulford premises in 1896.

No. 96 Queen Victoria St

This appears to have been a private house until Knavesmire Fisheries was listed in 1935, with Robert Nicholas, fishmonger and fish fryer. After the war it was Jim's Fisheries until around 1975. Then it became the Double Luck fish and chips and Chinese takeaway. Until recently it was South Bank Fisheries, but it closed around a year ago, and now is residential, with the display window bricked-up.

No. 98 Queen Victoria St

The shop here, still visible as a bricked-up window, was a butcher for a long time. In the 1920s it was George Boyes, pork butcher, then Frances Boyes from 1930. By 1951 it became Imeson's, then Archer's, then Crow Bros Ltd butchers, closing in 1971.

No. 99/101 Queen Victoria St

Again there are brickwork changes to this shop, remembered as double-fronted. No. 99 was Ernest Tebay's confectioners in the 1920s. Business must have been good as he expanded into no. 101 in 1927. Margaret Tebay was a retail dealer in tobacco, stationery and sweets in 1939. By 1951 it became Wardell's, then Herbert's, then Johnson's, then J & M Paton confectioners from 1959–1971. In the 1970s it was Janico

Queen Victoria St ca 1913, with new tramlines. (Mike Pollard)

Electrical Supplies, before they moved to 62/64 Balmoral Terrace. The shop closed in 1983.

No. 105 Queen Victoria St
This was briefly a baker's around 1913, run by Annie and Harold Windass.

No. 108 Queen Victoria St
With another now bricked-up shop window, this was R B and R M Douglas, draper and corsetière in 1939. She was the daughter of Mr and Mrs Tebay, who had a shop along the street. Intriguingly another Douglas, Lottie, was a corsetière at 40 South Bank Ave in the 1950s and 1960s.

After the war this was Fred Raw's hairdressers, lasting until 1986. Ian Shepherd told us that when he was very young, a haircut at Fred Raw's was always a threat from his mum, as Fred would pass a lit taper over the back of his neck, to 'seal his follicles'. It was renamed Harrison-Raw in 1963, and then the ladies' part moved to 74 Albemarle Rd. Christine's Chiropodist worked within the Harrison-Raw shop after this. It later became DG Associates and closed in 1997.

South Bank Ave

South Bank Ave was originally the driveway leading to Nunthorpe Hall (see page 37), described at the end of the 19th century as The Avenue, with a lodge for the Hall at the eastern end, on the corner of Bishopthorpe Rd. Work started on houses here in 1900 and Messrs De Burgh had a planning application for ten cottages in 'South Bank Avenue' in 1905. It was soon mostly complete on the south side, along with the name change. Houses on the north side were a much later construction, with the new Nunthorpe estate in the 1930s. David Meek's parents bought theirs at no.19 around 1936, when it was built, paying £425.

Surprisingly some of the gabled houses with bay windows and front forecourt gardens were shops for quite a while.

Houses for sale on the Nunthorpe estate in 1936, £595 for a semi-detached house with long garden. (Barbara Weatherley)

No. 1 South Bank Ave
Currently Vanilla Hair and Beauty

This was the first house on the right hand corner with Bishopthorpe Rd. In the late 1930s the Copley family, bakers, lived here, the start of a succession of bakers. John Copley appears to have become incapacitated, when his wife Lilian took over. After the war it was Henry Irwin, then Nora Watson. By 1967 it was J W Thompson baker, who shared the premises briefly in 1968 with Cheryl's ladies hairdresser. In the 1970s it was Newton's, lasting until the late 1980s. The single storey building next door to the shop was the actual bakery. This is now residential property.

Ironically in the 1990s it became Baker & Hudson computer consultants: 'IBM compatible and Archimedes with printer and accessories'. By 1996 though it was the Physical Therapy Clinic, with Wendy Keefer, LCSP, offering 'remedial massage, physical and sports therapy'. She was there till around 2005, and then by 2008 it was Chic

Look, hair stylists, nails, massage, beauty therapy. Elaine Simeon took over the business in 2012 and changed the name to Vanilla Hair and Beauty. As well as hair and beauty treatments Elaine offers chiropody and pedicures, as she completed the Scholl training in 1982.

No. 2 South Bank Ave

Photographs show the lodge building to Nunthorpe Hall on the southern corner of South Bank Ave as a newsagent's shop in the early 1930s. It was a small gabled building, with decorative pillars. A coachman, Charles Crane, lived here between 1885 and 1900, when it became vacant.

Posters in front of the newsagents on the 1930s photo highlight news stories such as: 'Missing Girl: Ghastly Story', 'Boy Trapped in Burning Train' and 'Death Drama in Yorkshire Hotel'. 'The Wolf Man' is showing at the City Picture Palace. The tramline fittings are visible.

The old lodge house for Nunthorpe Hall on the corner of South Bank Ave and Bishopthorpe Rd in the early 1930s, housing a newsagent. Note St Clement's Rectory on the left. (Hugh Murray)

John Hobson was listed as a grocer here in 1913, and then it was Miss Alice Holmes confectioner, followed by Fred Shuttleworth newsagent in the 1920s. The numbering becomes very confusing, as from 1926–1937 Shuttleworth's was listed here as 145 Bishopthorpe Rd, then it became no.131. After the war it was renumbered again, as no. 149, with first Frederick and then Hannah, his wife. (There appears to be a connection with Windsor St too in 1911). They must have been an elderly couple when running the newsagents, Fred died in 1928 and Hannah in 1937.

The Lodge was demolished around the late 1930s, possibly after Hannah's death, but the big house, Nunthorpe Hall, remained until 1977.

No 21 South Bank Ave

There was a retail milk deliverer here in 1939, George Parkin, whose father was a dairyman at 19 Ebor St. George remained at this address for a long time, but was no longer listed as a milk deliverer.

No 38 South Bank Ave

In 1939 there was a ladies' hairdresser here, Albert Rhodes. He had been at this address since the 1920s, but it was not clear how long he was in business as a hairdresser.

No 40 South Bank Ave

This was home to the Douglas family from the 1920s until the 1960s, Arthur and his wife Lottie. She was recorded as a corsetière in 1953, and soon after it was Mrs B Douglas corsetière. The business closed in 1967.

'Mrs. Douglas had a shop (no. 40) which sold ladies' corsets, bulletproof vests and foundation garments.' *(Derrick Gray).*

No. 44 South Bank Ave

This was Cairn's Hairdressers from around 1933. In 1939, Robert and Phyllis Cairns shared the ladies' and gents' clientele. By 1949 they also had a shop at 42 The Shambles, known as the Tudor Beautie Shoppe, later Cairns Hairdressing salon and coffee bar.

When Robert Cairns died in 1971, his obituary noted that he was the first man locally to demonstrate the cold wave (permanent waving). He had been provincial master of Leeds and District Branch of the Incorporated Guild of Hairdressers, Wigmakers and Perfumiers in 1950. He was a founder member of the Fellowship of Hair Artists of Great Britain, and a member of the International Brotherhood of

Magicians. He was politically active too, having been selected as a Conservative candidate for the Holgate Ward in 1955.

By 1951 this address was Wilde's Wool Store, with Herbert and Mrs G Wilde, closing in 1990.

'Although wool was her primary sales, she also sold sanitary towels from under the counter. You would be sent to get some and, only if no one was in the tiny shop (she worked it out of her front room), she would retrieve them and wrap them in brown paper to disguise them.' *(Christine B).*

No. 54 South Bank Ave
In 1939 this was Amy Hunter, milliner shopkeeper. By the 1950s it had changed to Ashman's grocery, then Long's, Beech's, and Simpson's. It became a hairdresser's, Cheryl's, in the late 1960s (Cheryl seems to have started off at 1 South Bank Avenue in 1968). Later it became Susan's Hair Fashion, Virginia's Hair Fashion, South Bank Salon, then Brian's Hair Fashions from around 1990, with the shop changing from a ladies' hairdressers to unisex. Brian has just retired and the shop has closed after 30 years.

No. 58/60 South Bank Ave
Currently York Evangelical Church

Harry Lacey was listed as a newsagent here in 1905, followed by Curtis and Hill grocers in 1909. In 1911 John Hobson was a general dealer here. He lasted until around 1932, at no. 60, and then in 1933 no. 58 became F N Scott fruiterer and grocer, spreading into no. 60 in the late 1940s. By 1975 it was F J Colley, grocer, eventually closing in 1985.

In more recent times this building has been bought by York Evangelical Church for use as church offices, flats and a community space. The doorway to no. 60 has a decorative brick framing.

No. 88a South Bank Ave
No 88a was originally the South Bank Mission Chapel, built in 1900 as an outreach centre for St. Clement's in Scarcroft Rd. It was a multi-purpose building which functioned as a place of worship before St. Chad's was built in 1925/6, and still retains a memorial stone. It was also used as a temporary school by 1906, which closed in 1916 and

Knavesmire Glass in South Bank Avenue, 2007. (Keith Watson)

moved to new premises as Knavesmire School. There was a Sunday School here in 1931, and it was also used for Mothers' Union meetings.

It became a warehouse, with William Henry Clarke from the 1930s. From the 1950s it was also used by Rowntree's to store the colourings to make sweets such as fruit pastilles. From 1967 it was Modern Glaziers, glass manufacturers, then Knavesmire Glass from 1987 for around ten years, and as a result it was known locally as the Glass Warehouse. It was converted to a private house around seven years ago.

'Both my brother Gerald and I attended Mothers' Union gatherings here until we started school. It was a rather dark and dingy place with a fireplace each side of the long walls, and a bit of a stage at the far end. The Mothers' Union at that time was in the charge of the Misses Argles, who incidentally produced and acted in plays. I can particularly remember Mrs. Mowbray, who usually played a man's role, often a comic one.'
(Derrick Gray).

No. 108 South Bank Ave

At the end of the terrace this was a grocer and confectioner in 1939, Florence Prest, although Walter Prest had been listed as living there since 1929. By 1949 it was Milner's, and then Smith's in the mid-1950s, closing in 1959.

The Nunthorpe estate

'Access to this field was by a five-barred gate just about where the road is now. Most of the time cattle grazed in this field, and the occasional horse. But its most memorable occasion to me was the Sunday School day out, where games and sports etc. took place. The highlight of the afternoon was the picnic tea. The arrival of Barton's Van was greeted with mixed feelings. I remember that each child received a bag of buns – 'Barton's bouncers' they were known as, drop one of these on your foot at your peril!' *(Derrick Gray).*
'My father remembered going to Scarcroft School over these fields in the early 1930s, using the gate and passing the large pond which was about halfway across. There were swans living on the pond at that time. It was later filled in as part of the building of the Estate, allegedly using stonework from York Castle which was being demolished in 1935. There also appear to be many of these large old square stones still scattered in many of the gardens on the estate.' *(Keith Watson).*

During the 1930s an estate of red brick semis was built on the area of open land between Southlands Rd and South Bank Ave, and the Winning Post pub opened. While traditional terraced housing suited shops, with many front windows opening directly onto the street, the design of the Nunthorpe estate did not cater for shop premises, as these were semi-detached houses with front gardens. Similarly later houses were built on the site of the old St Clement's Rectory, now Rectory Gardens.

Nunthorpe Grove has been described as the most ill-fated street in wartime York. In many parts it had not been possible to erect Anderson shelters, because there had been allotments and a pond on the site before the houses were built, and much of the ground was waterlogged, making it unsuitable. On 29 April 1942 a bomb dropped on nos. 23 and 25, destroying these, as well as nos.19 and 21. Several people were badly injured, and the body of a young ATS girl, Dorothy Thompson, was later found at the bottom of a bomb crater in no.21. Further bombs landed on other parts of the estate, between the houses. The houses were rebuilt in 1946.

In another devastating incident, on 5 March 1945, Halifax bombers from the Canadian 426 Squadron at Linton-on-Ouse took off to raid the German city of Chemnitz. These aircraft suffered from severe icing

Nunthorpe Grove had the reputation of being the unluckiest street in York in WWII. In 1942 a German bomb dropped on the street, and in 1945 a plane which had taken off from Linton-on-Ouse crashed on the street, due to severe icing. (Hugh Murray)

and three crashed soon after take-off. One broke up under the weight of ice which had accumulated on it, and its fuselage crashed on nos. 26 and 28 Nunthorpe Grove, killing two elderly ladies, while one of the engines hit the nearby school. The aeroplane carried eight bombs. Eleven people died – six of the crew and five civilians – and another 18 were injured in the crash. Four houses were set on fire.

Sutherland St

The first few houses here were built in 1913, at the east end of the street, with private street works for tarmacking and drainage for the new houses carried out a few years later.

No.8 Sutherland St
No. 8 was the last house on Sutherland St, on the corner with Count de Burgh Terrace. In 1913 it was Martha Corrighan's shop, and then in the 1920s it was George Corrighan, then Anna Bell general dealer. By the 1930s it was A E Heselwood, grocer. In the 1950s it became A E Chalk, radio engineer, who closed in 1970.

No.35 Sutherland St
This housed a taxicab proprietor J M & J W Sanderson, in the 1960s.

Trafalgar St
The street was built in stages from 1900, and initially directories show houses to the north of the junction with Balmoral Terrace. Later there were a few houses on the east side south of this junction, built around 1932. Private street works for tarmacking and drainage for the new houses were carried out in 1919. In 1934 Relton Bros builders started building work on the lower end houses, on land purchased from the De Burgh estate.

'My father remembered a smallholding on this patch of land, which had pigs and hens run by someone called Mothersdale around 1933.'
(Keith Watson).

The Trafalgar Street area had a surprising number of shops. Almost all of them were on the even side (east), and they mostly closed in the 1960s and 1970s. There is now only the Chinese takeway still open.

No. 1/3 Trafalgar St

These houses first appear in directories in the 1930s, with R. Bough boot repairer at no. 1. In the 1950s he was still there, upstairs, joined by Ronald Bough turf commission agent on the ground floor. By 1963 the boot repairer's had closed and it was just Ronald Bough, who seems to have spread to no. 3 too at that point. Bough's bookmakers closed in 1975.

'At 1/3 Trafalgar St, there was a cobblers called Bough's. He used to open a bookies on the side at the back, well it was illegal, then it became legal and he did more booking than cobbling.' *(David Meek)*

No. 24 Trafalgar St
Currently the Golden Horse Chinese takeaway

This is a very old shop, listed as a fried fish shop run by Arthur Dalby in 1905, followed by Fred Shuttleworth in 1909, and in 1911, run by Mary Oxley, while her husband worked as a North Eastern Railway carriage repairer, but listed as Tom Oxley's. By 1925 it was Fred Arnett's, until 1937, when it became Fred Kendrick fried fish dealer, who lasted until the 1970s, when was Dave's Fish & Chip Shop.

'At no 24 we had Arnett's – yet another fish and chip shop, making three within 100 yards, as well as Malarkey's. As I remember, 'one of each' cost 6d and were counted a treat, ours were usually home-made.' *(Derrick Gray)*.

No. 28 Trafalgar St
This building does not appear on the listings until 1961, when it was L Bardy's turf commission agent, lasting until 1974.

No. 30 Trafalgar St
There was a coal merchant here, from the turn of the 20th century. First Richard Air in 1901–1905, then William Johnson in 1909, then Edwin Turner Hebdon from 1913 until around 1940. His widow lived at this house for many years after.

No. 32 Trafalgar St
Richard Blyth Webster was a general dealer here in 1936.

No. 35 Trafalgar St
This was Seymour and Stacey fruiterers in the 1950s, later Thomas Seymour, trading on his own account. Their business used a horse and

cart, delivering door to door, with a stables in Cherry St. It closed in 1967.

'This was Seymour's groceries and sweets. Mrs. Seymour made all her own pickles and to me the shop smelt delicious! Mr. Seymour also had a grocery round with a horse and cart.' *(Derrick Gray).*

No.38 Trafalgar St
Henry Sharp was a 'coal hawker' here in 1901, trading until 1939, when it became coal merchant J Stephenson, who appeared to be briefly a turf commission agent in 1953. In 1955 it was Windsor & Co turf commission agents. The bookies closed in 1957.

No.42 Trafalgar St
This was briefly another coal dealer in 1911, John Ormsby. From the 1930s it was Thomas Seymour, general dealer, who seems to have taken the opportunity to move across to no. 35 in 1953. After he left here it was Oddy's, then Mrs Emily Smith, then Mrs M Atkinson, then Mrs Goodrick in the 1960s, before closing in 1967.

Knavesmire Tuck Shop at 42 Trafalgar St in the 1950s, with Emily Powell. (Clare Bryant)

Clare Bryant provided a lovely photo of her great-grandmother Emily Powell, outside her tuck shop here around 1953. Local residents recall that they called into the shop from Knavesmire Infants. 'They used to get a 3d bit in their pudding at the school Christmas dinner and be taken down there a class at a time to spend it.'

No.44 Trafalgar St
This was Frank Allington's wet fishmonger from the late 1930s, closing in 1967. It was one of several fishmongers on South Bank, many opening up their front rooms to sell fish.

Westwood Terrace
A De Burgh planning application for 20 houses in 1900 was approved and houses were in the course of construction at the Albemarle Road end by 1909. Building further along the terrace started around 1915, and private street works for tarmacking and drainage for the new houses was carried out in 1919. At the eastern end Relton Bros builders began building new semi-detached houses in 1932, on land purchased from the De Burgh estate.

We have been told that long ago there were regular fairs here, such as a traditional Michaelmas Fair held at the bottom of the terrace, including wild animals in cages.

No. 74 Westwood Terrace
This house was recorded as R & M Douglas(s) drapers between 1936 and 1938, who may have been connected to the other Douglas(s) traders in Queen Victoria St and in South Bank Ave. By 1939 it was a fruiterer and market gardener, Charles Sheppeard, with Frank Sheppeard and Lily Sheppeard shopkeeper. Sheppeard's were there until 1970, when it became M E Ellan, fruiterer. This shop was absorbed into the bookies at 139 Albemarle Rd.

Finally, the eastern edge of our area featured a range of shops from the early days, on Bishopthorpe Rd itself and also on Finsbury St, near the river, a surprising hive of trading.

Bishopthorpe Rd
The 1907 map shows that development along here from the centre of York ended at Southlands Rd on the west side and just after Richardson St on the east side. But there were a few blocks of houses further down,

around Butcher Terrace and Beresford Terrace on the east side, and between Balmoral Terrace and Campleshon Lane on the west side.

The Little House, 76A Bishopthorpe Rd

This is a quirky house, frequently referred to as the 'smallest house in York', now a tiny holiday home, but formerly the surgery for the local doctor who lived next door, which is now occupied by the owner. The photograph on page 96 shows how tiny the house was, and still is.

In 1925 the doctor at no.76 was James Lawther, followed by Harry Taylor in 1933. In 1963 it was Alex Reid, physician and surgeon, and then in 1975 it was JK Gosnold, physician and surgeon.

No. 127/129 Bishopthorpe Rd
Winning Post Public House

The Winning Post opened on 22 May 1939, built by John Smith & Sons, after the licence from the Red Lion in Micklegate was transferred to it. At the same time the licence from the former pub The Sportsman in Caroline St was forfeited. This followed a long period of temperance agitation, led by Canon Argles of St Clement's. He had arrived in the parish in 1871 and became an outspoken critic of drinking and public houses, seeing drink as a social evil. Despite the large number of houses being built in the Bishopthorpe Rd area of York he was able to use his influence to prevent pubs opening in South Bank while he was alive. His influence lived on after he died in 1920, and it was not until 1932 that the Knavesmire pub opened.

The Winning Post was a popular pub with a large function room, becoming famous for many bands appearing there. Shed Seven played their first public gig here in 1990. The York Punk band Cyanide also played here. There were some great old characters too, such as 'Mad Albert'.

In 1970 John Smith's Brewery was taken over by Courage, who were taken over themselves in 1995 by their rivals Scottish & Newcastle. In turn they were taken over by Heineken in 2008. By the 1990s however the structure of pub ownership had changed, and pub-owning companies were set up ('pubcos'), splitting off from breweries. The Winning Post is now owned by EI Publican Partnerships, formerly Enterprise Inns.

The Little House on Bishopthorpe Rd, to the right of no.76, squeezed into the gap. (YAYAS)

'Mad Albert' and the York punk band Cyanide, in the Winning Post ca 1977.

The pub became rather run-down and by 2014 there were concerns about the possibility of a large supermarket taking over the premises, with its effect on independent traders, as well as the loss of one of the only two pubs in the area. As a result, after an application by local traders, it was listed in 2014 as an asset of community value to protect it from development.

In December 2015, new managers Malcolm and Fiona Tolladay took over, with an ambitious and extensive programme of renovation. They were fascinated to find under the floor some interesting racing-related decorative features – a horse and jockey and a horseshoe motif.

It is now a successful pub and community resource, with many regular events in its rooms, such as the Comedy Club, Gin Club, musical events, art exhibitions and cinema nights. Fiona plays a big part in the Bishopthorpe Rd Traders Association too.

'The Winning Post, before it was built, it must have been before the war, I remember going there, it was a sort of a big empty space, and there was a marquee on it and I think all the people round about went to sort of a party to celebrate something. And it must have been the Coronation, would it be Queen Elizabeth and King George VI? We all had street parties and that was where they had the Bishopthorpe Rd area street party. I had my wedding reception there, in 1952, about 80 guests, yes a buffet and so it must have been one of the big rooms. I just remember the people, a very nice family. I remember June Anstead. I'm not sure whether she didn't do a bit of modelling. She was a very attractive young lady.' *(Jean Potts)*.

St Clement's Rectory
St. Clement's Church Rectory was on Bishopthorpe Rd, between South Bank Ave and Balmoral Terrace, a large house well away from the church, in fields to the south of York. Plans were drawn up by York architect Herbert Fippard in 1867 and contractors appointed in 1869. In 1871 Canon George Marsham Argles was appointed first Rector of the combined parish of St Mary Bishophill Senior with St. Clement's and became the first occupant of the Rectory when it was completed in 1872.

There were plans for re-draining and sanitary improvements at the Rectory in 1911 and for further improvements in 1918. In 1919

Rev Canon Argles retired and was replaced by Rev. Gilbert David Barker. The Rectory was demolished in 1936 to make way for new houses, in a new cul-de-sac named Rectory Gardens.

St Clement's Rectory on Bishopthorpe Road, now Rectory Gardens.

Cameron Walker Homes
Also known as Walker Barstow Homes and Cameron Walker Court

Charles Cameron Walker was a member of the Cameron brewing family, who died in 1907. His almshouses were established in Bishopthorpe Rd in 1909, and became a registered charity in 1912, with an endowment of £6,250. The northern gable end is inscribed with the date 1912 in the brickwork. They comprised twelve three-room dwellings in a two storied building designed by Walter Brierley, described by Pevsner as 'Tudor-style, red brick with stone details and mullioned windows'. The almshouses were declared open to the poor of either sex living within 10 miles of York. The building had three doorways, each opening onto a hall with two flats on each of the two floors. The flats were built with a living room with a range and oven, and a separate bedroom. There was a narrow scullery with sink and cold water tap and a small gas ring and grill. The wash-house was in the garden and contained two coppers, two sinks, cold water taps and mangles. Each pair of flats shared a WC, but there were no baths installed when the house was built. Electric light, installed from the beginning, and water were provided free.

The twelve original residents included two couples (one of whom was the caretaker and spouse). The others were widows or spinsters. The inmates' stipends were fixed in 1912 at 5s. per week for single people, and 8s. for married couples. In 1946, 5s. 6d. per week was being paid.

To qualify for housing as a beneficiary of the trust applicants must be an adult or an adult couple, living within a 10 mile radius of the centre of York and have limited financial means. It is also a condition of living at the almshouses that residents must be capable of independent living.

Barstow's Hospital in Caroline St was demolished in the 1960s, and in 1972 the charity was merged with Cameron Walker Homes to become Walker Barstow Homes. A warden's bungalow and two others for residents were added at this time. In 1980 1 Aldreth Grove was bought and converted into flats. Modernisation of the main block was carried out in 1982, adding a bathroom to each dwelling. A communal lounge, known as the Barstow Lounge, was added in 1993, and in 1996 a house in Cameron Grove was purchased and converted into two more dwellings. The almshouses now house nineteen residents, with a 24-hour warden call system.

Cameron Walker Homes on Bishopthorpe Rd, 1915. (YAYAS)

No. 145 Bishopthorpe Rd

Currently Charles Symington Bookbinders.

This part of Bishopthorpe Rd is a little confusing. Between 1920 and 1925 there was nothing listed in directories between nos 95 and 157. Then from 1926 until 1937 there was a no.145, Shuttleworth's newsagents, almost certainly then the lodge house on the corner of South Bank Avenue. In 1938, a large number of houses and some shops in directories appeared in this gap, and the current property, a semi-detached house, was listed as 145 for the first time. It had been bought by Alice Jane Parkin in 1937 from the estate developers Harry and Louise Williamson, to enable her to run a dairy here, Nunthorpe Dairy, and the adjacent workshop was built in the plot next door. After the war it was, until 1961, Cyril Foster, jeweller, who had moved from Montague St. He must have been a prominent figure locally, selected as liberal candidate for the Knavesmire Ward in 1938. In the 1960s it was L. Leavitt cycle dealer, later cycle repairs. Later again it was a children's clothes shop, then Telemarine TV, Graphic Reproduction, and Securihome in the late 1980s.

Charles Symington and his wife Gill bought no.145 in 1992. Charles is a restoration bookbinder, restoring the binding on old volumes for clients over a wide area. He learned his craft from his father Douglas Symington, working in Low Petergate and then Coffee Yard, before moving to a workshop at Hospital Fields.

Charles is the grandson of John Alexander Symington, who created the Brotherton Collection of rare books and manuscripts in his spare time, as librarian to the industrialist Lord Brotherton. He was also Keeper of the Collection at the University of Leeds, curator of the Brontë Parsonage Museum, and edited the Shakespeare Head Brontë. Charles tells us that his grandfather was juggling several jobs at the same time, including writing books and being manager of the Leeds Labour Exchange at the time.

No. 147 Bishopthorpe Rd

Currently Tower Veterinary Group

This first appears in 1938 as W J Hannon, fruiterer, later in 1957 it became H Shortle, florist, and by the 1970s a fruiterer and greengrocer.

It was then George King's fruiterers, then in 1983 The Flower Shop, and 1994 it was Job's Fruit & Veg. In 1997 it became Abbeyfields Veterinary Clinic, now absorbed by Tower Veterinary Group. Tower Vets originated in Sutton-on-the-Forest in the 1950s.

No. 147a Bishopthorpe Rd
Currently Knaresborough Kitchens

This is a newer, single storey building, constructed in the space between nos. 145 and 147 in the 1980s. It was Bygones Antiques, then Kestrel Printers, then Eperon Doors. In 2003 it became South Bank Kitchens, who were taken over by Knaresborough Kitchens in 2012. They are a family-run business which started in Knaresborough in 1996.

No. 148 Bishopthorpe Rd
On the opposite side of Bishopthorpe Rd, on the corner of Cameron Grove, there was a chemist's for a long time. In 1928 it was Cyril Davies' drugstore, later retitled C & E Davies Ltd, and still there in 1939. After the war it was a York Co-operative Society chemist until 1968. It later became Lockwood's Laundrette, and then The Washeteria, then The Tanning Room, before closing.

No. 149 Bishopthorpe Rd
(See also 2 South Bank Ave).This building on the south east corner of South Bank Avenue appears in directories as no. 145, from 1927 until 1937, with Fred Shuttleworth running a newsagents here, for a long period. It is confusing because 2 South Bank Avenue was also there. It was commonly known as 'Shutts', and unusually open on Sundays. In 1938 it reappears as no. 131, a newsagent run by Hilda Coughlin, who was Fred Shuttleworth's daughter, then by 1949 it became no.149, still Coughlin's. Hilda's husband John was a jobbing builder on South Bank. In 1955 it became Tacey's and in 1972 Haw's. In 1988 it was Clark's newsagent, before eventually closing, with a newsagency moving across to the corner of Butcher Terrace in 2010.

No. 153 Bishopthorpe Rd
In 1939 this was a hairdresser, Amy Cattle, listed until 1961, although the Cattle family continued to live there from that time onwards.

No. 162 Bishopthorpe Rd
Currently Village Spice

This is at the junction with Butcher Terrace, leading to the river. In the very early days it was XL Supply Stores, who had another branch on the corner of Darnborough St, until recently the old antique shop. From 1909 this corner shop was Thomas Knowles, a baker, grocer and confectioner, who lasted until around 1937. After the war it was T. W. Brown, with the Glen Park Bakery, which became the Glen Park Library in 1953. (Another shop with this name was in Heworth at 67 East Parade). In 1959 it became Swiers Butchers, who also had a shop in Tang Hall Lane. Ken Hodgson took over in 1967.

Dennis Job moved to York in 1978 from Middlesbrough and worked with Ken Hodgson. As well as meats they made their own burgers and sold tripe, and added home-made pastries to their shop. Dennis became a partner and took over when Ken died in 1985, living above the shop.

'Gradually we started to sell sausage rolls, steak and kidney pies, mince and onion pies and pork pies, then chicken and mushroom quiches. The pastry side did really well. I took the business from the shop across the road (Nunthorpe Bakery in South Bank Avenue), which was closing down in the late 1980s. I took on much of the catering equipment from Nunthorpe Bakery and used it on my premises for my pastries and pies.' (Dennis Job).

Dennis also took on the greengrocers' business across the road, but it was not successful, and trade was suffering in Butcher Terrace. There was no longer a through route for motorists into town along Terry Avenue, Tesco's had opened their superstore in Tadcaster Road and there were also concerns about BSE at this time. He moved away from the shop in the 1990s, taking on Mr Galloway to run it, then Paul Statham. Eventually Dennis sold the business around 1995 and it became the Bay of Bengal Indian Restaurant/Takeaway around 1997. It is now the Village Spice.

'There was a private library. You used to be able to borrow books for about 1d a book. The place was full of books and a bit dusty. Because you see in those days, I think we had a radio but you didn't have television, and you read an awful lot. Then after that it became a butcher's, Ken Hodgson, he was a smashing fella, a good butcher, a really kind man. He looked after people. I remember when my auntie lost her husband, she went into the butcher's and he said 'Can I have a word with you?' and he took her into the back and he said 'I'm sorry that Mr Coates has died, I really am, and if you only want one sausage Mrs Coates, you come and ask for it. And if it's raining, send a message and we'll deliver it for you.' Butchers, it was a skilled trade. I remember Ken saying, these butchers in the supermarkets, they aren't butchers, they're meat chopperuppers.' *(David Meek)*.

The corner of Butcher Terrace and Bishopthorpe Rd around 1900, with the XL Supply Stores, who also had a shop on the corner of Darnborough St, which later became the antique shop. (Peter Stanhope)

No. 162a Bishopthorpe Rd
Currently Millennium Food & Wine

The northern corner of Butcher Terrace was a grocer's as early as 1909, run by Louisa Mold, an unfortunate name for a grocer. In the 1920s there were three different grocers, Downey's, Moore's and then Sturdy's. In the 1930s it was William Swales, then Hines, who was there until the 1950s. By 1959 it was J Harrison, who was there until at least the 1970s. R M Ferry was the grocer in the 1980s, followed by M Shafiq. In the 1990s it was Annabelle's, then R & K General Store, then The Cove, then Pat's Place between 1999 and 2004. It is now Millennium Food and Wine and still open. It provides a very useful source of alcohol for customers at the Village Spice opposite.

'There was a grocer's at the corner of Butcher Terrace called Hines. It was a father and son that ran it, and when I came home from school, I think it was a Wednesday, my mum used to put the dinner on and I used to go down with a book with all the groceries in. And she used to give me a pound note and a ten shilling note and there was always change. And I often think about this every time I go to the supermarket, she'd put 'a pound of cheese' and they'd say, 'oh does your mum want red or white?' That was the choice that you had! Then, later on when I got to about 11 or 12, I used to go down there in the holidays and used to help, and used to cut the cheese up, and the butter, you wouldn't be allowed now, would you? And we used to bag sugar up into blue bags and the first day you went you used to keep putting in a little bit, but then you know how much to put on the shovel and it was 2lb. Deliveries by carrier bike…sometimes he came the same day, he used to pedal up on the bike and he had a big cardboard box, he used to load it all onto your kitchen unit and take the cardboard box away again. He also sold draught paraffin and draught vinegar, and they were side by side. He would fill up these bottles and say, don't get them mixed up! The whole place smelled of paraffin and vinegar and nice things. Of course they didn't have fridges in those days.'
(David Meek).

'Around the corner from the vinegar man on Bish Rd was a bike shop, where a man custom-made bikes from used and new parts or just sold used bikes. It reverted to private use likely in the 60s. I was given a new adult bike from there when I was 11 and I used it until my mid-20s and then gave it back to my Dad.' (Christine Strudstrup.)

No. 175 Bishopthorpe Rd
Currently South Bank Medical Centre

South Bank Medical Centre was created around 1989, with the merger of this address with no. 2 Balmoral Terrace as one address, and the transfer of the practice from no.12 Balmoral Terrace.

Butcher Terrace

John Thomas Wood had applied for planning permission for four cottages in Butcher Terrace in 1903 and the 1907 map shows a number of houses here, especially on the south side. It was possibly named after the York MP John Butcher, who was given the freedom of the city in 1906, when he finished his first term as MP.

No. 1 Butcher Terrace

A grocer was listed here in 1902, William Burns Honeyburn.

Finsbury St

Finsbury St crosses Butcher Terrace, parallel to the River Ouse. John Thomas Wood applied for planning permission for twelve houses here during 1901/3. It was a centre of trading activity for much of the period between the 1930s and 1970s. There would have been as many as five shops or traders here, and a couple of older shops had closed down.

House building extended into Finsbury Ave in 1936.

No. 2 Finsbury St

Sidney Wilson was listed with a dairy here in 1913.

No. 6 Finsbury St

This also housed a dairyman for many years. From 1935 it was Harry Lancaster, helping poorer locals by selling cracked eggs. Then by 1955 it was William Whitely, closing in 1974.

No. 15 Finsbury St

This was a boot and shoe repairer for many years, Cecil Hide was recorded as a bootmaker in 1911, closing in 1953. Mr Hide was renowned for talking with a mouthful of tacks.

No. 17 Finsbury St

Grocers traded here for many years. From 1909 it was Elizabeth Wrightson and then by 1921 Robert Harper Wrightson, with Edith May Wrightson in 1933. In 1939 it was Arthur Alderson. After the war the grocer was N Tillott in 1949, followed by E Tillott until 1961. In the mid-1960s it was P & J Wedgwood grocers, closing in 1967.

'Edie Wrightson sold everything. She had pinnies and tea towels hanging up in there for sale. If people wanted credit they told her to 'put it down'.' *(Barbara Weatherley).*

No. 40 Finsbury St

Yet another master dairyman was listed here in 1939, Charles F Howell, but the Howell family had been at this address listed as residents since around 1911, so they may have been trading for a long time before 1939. Howell's eventually closed in 1978. A photograph shows them delivering milk using a motor bike and sidecar.

Howell's dairy offered an unusual form of delivery from no 40 Finsbury St, in the 1920s. (Geoff Shearsmith).

No. 42 Finsbury St

This was Nicholson's mobile fruit/veg van in the 1960s, closing in 1981.

No. 61 Finsbury St

J N Hudson was a bootmaker here in 1900.

No. 66 Finsbury St

In the 1901 census there was a grocer listed here, Mary Driver, but directories record Joseph F. Driver as the shopkeeper from 1900–1905.

No. 67 Finsbury St
Mary Blacker was a shopkeeper here in 1905.

No. 68 Finsbury St
In 1939 there was a grocer listed here, Arthur Fratson.

No. 70 Finsbury St
Alfred Henry Wood was a shopkeeper here in 1902.

Rowntree Park

Joseph Rowntree's gift of a park to the people of York was his tribute
to the 200 workers of Rowntree Cocoa Works who died or suffered
in WW1. The Park was built on Nun Ings, approximately 20 acres of
water meadow, which he bought from the council. Designed by Arts
and Crafts architects Fred Rowntree and W J Swain, it was York's first
municipal park. Originally it included bowling greens, an outdoor
swimming pool, aviaries, a tearoom and snack bar, and a bandstand
for a full orchestra.

The lych gate with its dovecote symbolises peace. A bronze memorial
plaque in the arch expresses gratitude to the fallen and places hope in
the League of Nations, the first international organisation for world
peace, founded in 1920. The white garden fantail doves are believed to
be direct descendants of the original peace doves of 1921.

In 1954, as a World War II memorial the Rowntree factory donated the
iron entrance gates on Terry Avenue, and a second bronze plaque was
added to the lych gate.

The park is owned by the council but the Friends of Rowntree Park is
a voluntary group which seeks to promote the well-being of the Park
and its users, carrying out some practical tasks, such as gardening
and maintenance. The Friends also run a wide range of events and
activities for the community.

The area to the south of Beresford Terrace, on the east side of
Bishopthorpe Rd, has changed considerably over the years. There
are now semi-detached and detached houses, built in the 1950s, and

further south there are newer flats. But all of this area was once the site of four very large houses accommodating well-known York families, taking advantage of the picturesque riverside, with a long history.

Old Nunthorpe

'Nunthorpe' or 'Old Nunthorpe' was used as a name for this group of houses at different times, as well as the general area, so it can be confusing. But looking at the houses in turn we can summarise what we know of the puzzle of their history.

Starting from where Beresford Terrace is now, the first house (on a site now occupied by a line of 1950s houses) was originally built in the 1830s, for the Lawton family. Other names mentioned in the 1830s and 1840s were Captain Young, the Ord family and James Scupham. Around 1850 that house was demolished and two Victorian semi-detached villas built, known as Nunthorpe or Nun Thorpe. George Lawton owned these. He was one of the proctors of the Ecclesiastical Courts of York, and lived in the northernmost house. He rented out the southern house to the Wade family in 1861. George was succeeded as landowner by William Lawton. In 1891 the southern house was rented out to Wilfrid Forbes Home Thomson (1858–1939), a York banker, for £70 a year. It was big, the 1911 census records it as having 23 rooms. Wilfrid was a partner in the York firm of Beckett & Co, bankers, and was created 1st Baronet of Old Nunthorpe in 1925 for 'political and public services in York'. He was the eldest son of the Most Reverend William Thomson, Archbishop of York from 1862 to 1890. Mrs Thomson played Lady Fairfax in the 1909 York Pageant.

At times this house was described as the 'White House' in directories.

In 1900 the council bought riverside land from Captain Lawton and from Mr Proctor (see Ashcroft) to complete a much needed riverside walk from Clementhorpe. In 1902 William Lawton died and there was a sale of the two houses and grassland around the site, and T.F. Wood bought the Thomson house but the family stayed on. It may be that they also took over the northern house, as a report of a burglary in 1937 describes their house as one home with two entrances. In 1937

Two views of Old Nunthorpe on Bishopthorpe Rd in 1902. Above from the roadside, and below from the riverside. (Hugh Murray)

'Old Nunthorpe Hall' (and nearby fields), formerly the home of Sir Wilfred Thomson was sold for £1,800. He died in 1939.

In the 1930s developers had been starting to swarm, and in 1934 the brewery company John J Hunt Ltd advertised a 'Shopping Site corner on Bishopthorpe Rd and Beresford Terrace, South Bank York, area 700 square yards for sale'.

Old Nunthorpe was eventually demolished and replaced around the 1950s by the row of semi-detached and detached houses.

Riverside Lodge

The next house was on a site now occupied by new flats, Riverside Lodge, St Chad's Wharf and Terry Mews. This house was built around 1880, by Demaine and Brierley, and later became known as Riverside Lodge. Described by Pevsner as in 'red brick, with timber-framed and bargeboarded gables, pretty terracotta panels and friezes, and ironwork', it was greatly enlarged in 1897.

It was built for the Wood family, a famous timber merchant family associated with the river in York, who lasted there until around 1930, in a house with 11 rooms according to the 1911 census. Cecil Ernest Wood died in 1932 in Keswick, but by 1925 Francis Terry had moved into the Riverside Lodge, sometimes confusingly called Old Nunthorpe. By 1939 he had moved again to Middlethorpe Manor.

Riverside Lodge was then taken over by the Army as administrative offices, and a group of 1950s flats known as 'Old Nunthorpe House' was built on part of the original Riverside Lodge grounds for Army personnel. These were demolished in the 1990s.

In 1971 the house was bought by the Scurr family from the Territorial Army, for a hotel, and developed as the Sauna Health and Beauty Hotel, including La Riviera licensed restaurant. (The family also ran a firm of heating engineers, Scurr Heating Ltd, from this address, with premises at 24 Nunnery Lane and 1 Norfolk St.) The hotel was later renamed the Riverside Lodge Hotel, with a gym and pool. In later years it was the Riverside Lodge Nursing Home, managed by the Scurr family, but this closed in 1998, when trading conditions arising from government policy changes made independent homes less economic. Jeremy Scurr went on to run The Sidings Hotel and Restaurant outside York.

Permission was obtained to build 38 apartments on the site, and the York Archaeological Trust started excavations on the derelict site at 292 Bishopthorpe Rd, in advance of proposed redevelopment, The building was demolished and the flats were built, one group of which is still called Riverside Lodge.

Ashcroft

The southernmost of the four houses was Ashcroft, built in 1882 and described by Pevsner as having similar details to the Riverside Lodge. The architect was possibly Demaine or W H Thorpe. It was built on land bought from Archbishop of York's estate, the Ecclesiastical Commissioners, for John William Proctor, the managing director of Henry Richardson's Clementhorpe Tannery and Fertiliser Works beside Skeldergate Bridge. It was based on two and a quarter acres of land on the Ouse riverbank, and named Ashcroft House after a large ash tree in the grounds near the river.

In 1911 this house had 16 rooms. Proctor left in 1913 and rented the house out to the Dunnington-Jefferson family. It was bought by Francis Terry in 1925, as the new Terry factory was being built opposite. Although Francis Terry never lived in Ashcroft himself, several members of his family did from time to time. Francis lived next door.

In 1939 the RAF VR took it over. After Sir Francis Terry died the house was put up for sale in 1968, and bought by Geoff and Jean Woods and Robin Bell in 1970, opening as an hotel, the Ashcroft Hotel. It was later sold on to Les and Jan Granger in 1994. The location and size of the site led to interest in redevelopment, and planning was approved for demolition and the building of a new block of flats, with a terrace of houses facing the river behind. This happened in 2001.

No. 296 Bishopthorpe Rd

A workshop and offices for a printing firm, JW Bullivant & Sons, was here from 1973, opposite the Terry's factory. It was originally built as a garage by the Army, possibly in the 1950s and Bullivant's moved here from their previous premises in Stonegate. The building was demolished in 2013 after it had been partially destroyed by a large fallen tree. It has now been replaced by two town houses.

Terry's of York
Now The Chocolate Works and Springfield Care Village

In 1926 the York confectionery manufacturer Terry's moved from their factory in Clementhorpe to a purpose-built art deco style factory off Bishopthorpe Rd, alongside York Racecourse. The Clementhorpe factory remained in use by Terry's up to the 1980s, when its last use was for the storage of obsolete packaging before being demolished to make way for the Bishops Wharf development.

The new factory was a landmark building and some of their most famous brands were created here: the Chocolate Apple in 1926, All Gold in 1930 and the Chocolate Orange a year later. It was constructed between 1924 and 1926, designed by architect J. E. Wade and built by Dorman Long, including a 135 ft tall distinctive clock tower and the five-storey 510 ft long main factory building.

In 1937 there was a Royal visit by King George VI, Queen Elizabeth and Princess Elizabeth. During World War II, confectionery production was halted and the factory was taken over by F Hills and Sons of Manchester as a shadow factory, to manufacture and repair aircraft propeller blades.

Terry's was bought by Trust House Forte in 1963 then sold to Colgate Palmolive in 1977 then United Biscuits in 1982. United Biscuits sold their confectionery division to Kraft Foods in 1993, and Kraft amalgamated Terry's with Jacobs Suchard to create Terry's Suchard.

Sadly in 2004 the factory closure was announced, with production to be moved to other Kraft European factories. It ceased production in 2005, with the loss of 316 jobs.

In 2006 the £26m site was bought by Grantside Ltd and in 2010, after a long period of negotiation and consultation, a planning application was approved by York City Council. In 2013 the site was bought by joint developers Henry Boot Developments and David Wilson Homes, who have built apartments, penthouse suites and terraced housing.

In 2017 the original main office block, a Grade II listed building, re-opened as the Chocolate Works Care Village, created by Springfield Healthcare.

Bustardthorpe Allotments and George Russell

The success of an earlier allotment scheme at Holgate led York Corporation to advertise for other groups and individuals to petition for sites in the first decade of the 20th century. Our South Bank residents were the first to do so, but the authority had problems with identifying suitable land. The Smallholdings and Allotments Committee, which sat for the first time in January 1908, suggested to the newly formed South Bank Allotment Holders' Association that land at Bustardthorpe, behind the York Racecourse be considered.

At first the Association thought this was too far away from existing houses at that time. Despite this the Committee went ahead and in 1909 secured the land for 129 plots, in two fields at Bustardthorpe, 'for the labouring classes'. The rents were set at 12s 6d a year. The Association was renamed the Bishopthorpe Rd Allotment Association and began to organise shows for produce. At this time the Lord Mayor of York was its President and the Sheriff was Vice-President. Even the Archbishop of York was a member. This demonstrates that allotments had a major role to play in community life, as large areas of open space in York, especially near the riverside, were in private hands and inaccessible to the working classes.

In December 1916, to meet the need for expansion for wartime needs, the Committee considered a number of sites, including Hospital Fields (Albemarle Road), Upper Scarcroft, Beresford Terrace and Bishopthorpe Rd. They aimed to create around 470 allotment plots in total, each around 300 square yards. To meet food shortages they specified that two thirds should be for potatoes. In 1917 the Ancient Society of Florists agreed to give a prize for the highest yields from these allotments.

This move proved very popular, with 516 applications by January 1917. Local byelaws were suspended and people were allowed to keep pigs and chickens on plots, if properly housed. The Yorkshire Gazette claimed the allotment as an act of patriotism: 'We do not hesitate to say that the man who, knowing how to grow potatoes does not at once ask for land and get to work, will be as blameworthy as would the corporal who, seeing a chance to capture an army of the enemy, put off the effort until it was too late.' The local press saw the popularity of the new allotments as a weapon in defeating the U-boats.

In 1917 the National Government of David Lloyd George passed the Cultivation of Lands Order Act and York Corporation set up War Allotments throughout the city, including Albemarle Rd, Scarcroft Hill, Bishopthorpe Rd, Beresford Terrace, Knavesmire Crescent, Campleshon Lane, South Bank Ave and Thompson's Field. By now it was estimated that over 65 acres in total had been allocated to allotments, a tenth of the area of city, with 1,091 plots. This was estimated to be a greater proportion than any other northern city.

During World War II in 1943 new allotments started at the present Bustardthorpe site, and in 1961 the original allotments next to the Terry's site were closed, to make extra racecourse car parking, and allotment holders were moved over.

George Russell, who lived at 20 Kensington St in South Bank, was a jobbing gardener with an allotment at Bustardthorpe. He was inspired to start breeding better lupins in 1911 by the sight of a vase of lupins arranged by a Mrs Micklethwaite, one of his employers, at a house on The Mount. He noticed that her lupins were very poor and was convinced he could do better, so he embarked on a 20-year project to develop a new much improved strain.

He preferred natural pollination by bumble bees for hybridisation to vegetative propagation or hand pollination. At the end of each season he collected seed from the very best plants and sowed it. Any inferior plants were rigorously removed. He carried on until by the 1930s, with people travelling from across the country to see the lupins blooming in his Bishopthorpe Rd plot. By the 1940s every lupin sold was a Russell lupin and by the age of 79 he was exhibiting at Chelsea. His sturdy plants became a feature of the post-war garden, and each packet of seeds was sealed with his picture as a sign of authenticity.